MW00475111

Recreating
Antique Quilts
Re-envisioning, Modifying and Simplifying Museum Quilts
by Wendy Sheppard

Landauer Publishing, LLC

Recreating
Antique Quilts
by Wendy Sheppard

Copyright © 2014 by Landauer Publishing, LLC
Projects Copyright © 2014
by Wendy Sheppard

This book was designed, produced,
and published by Landauer Publishing, LLC
3100 101st Street, Urbandale, IA 50322
515/287/2144 800/557/2144 landauerpub.com

President/Publisher: Jeramy Lanigan Landauer
Vice President of Sales and Administration: Kitty Jacobson
Editor: Jeri Simon
Art Director: Laurel Albright
Photographer: Sue Voegtlin
Advertising and Marketing Manager: McB McManus
Digital Marketing Manager: E.B. Updegraff

All rights reserved. No part of this book may be reproduced or transmitted in any form
by any means, electronic or mechanical, including photocopying, recording, or by any
information storage and retrieval system without permission in writing from the publisher
with the exception that the publisher grants permission to enlarge the template patterns
in this book for personal use only. The scanning, uploading and distribution of this book
or any part thereof, via the Internet or any other means without permission from the
publisher is illegal and punishable by law. The publisher presents the information in this
book in good faith. No warranty is given, nor are results guaranteed.

Library of Congress Control Number: 2014937728

ISBN 13: 978-1-935726-63-0

This book printed on acid-free paper.
Printed in United States

10-9-8-7-6-5-4-3-2-1

 FACEBOOK.COM/
LANDAUERPUBLISHING
 YOUTUBE.COM/
LANDAUERPUBLISHING
 PINTEREST.COM/
LANDAUERPUB

Dedication

This book is dedicated to my 5-year-old daughter, Gwendolyn.
It is my hope that she will also discover the joy of needle and thread.

Calico Trail Quilt

Ginkgos on Prince Street Pillow

Priscilla's Garden Party Quilt
Garden Lattice Quilt

Oh, Happy Stars! Quilt

Stars & Snowflakes Table Topper

Feathery Formation Quilt

Patches & Crosses Table Runner

Floral Fancy Wallhanging

Ivory Baltimore Wallhanging

Table of Contents

About the Author

My interest in quilts was born out of my love for early and colonial American history. Being from Southeast Asia, my exposure to quilts was minimal due to the fact that quilt making is mainly a Western fabric art. Through reading I became enamored with the look of Baltimore Album quilts, but since I didn't know how to sew they seemed beyond my ability.

Years later, with repeated encouragement from my dear friend Barbara, I decided to give quilting a try. My main goal was to "share" a quilting experience with the women I read about in history. In 2005 without any prior sewing experience, I made my first quilt. My second, third and fourth quilt quickly followed.

Being totally naive, I submitted my fourth quilt for a magazine editorial feature. It was accepted. Since then, my work has been featured in domestic and overseas quilting publications. I also design projects for a variety of fabric companies in the quilting industry. My training and work experience as a chemical engineer have helped me strive for excellence (and more often than not, precision) in my quilt designs.

As a quilter, I am passionate about discovering and adapting historical and antique quilts for today's quilters. I quilt 99 percent of my quilts on my domestic sewing machine. I have shared my love of quilting with others by teaching an online "Learn to Machine Quilt" class. I also enjoy speaking at meetings where I have the opportunity to meet quilters who inspire me.

These days, I live with my family in northern Virginia where I juggle quilting and taking care of my five-year-old daughter. When I am not quilting, I enjoy reading biographies or something historical, browsing through catalogs, smocking and doing heirloom needlework.

To learn more, visit www.wendysheppard.net.

Floral Fancy Wallhanging, page 78

Introduction

I have always been fascinated by antique quilts - even when I did not know how to quilt, or had not caught the quilting bug. I can imagine the makers of these masterpieces persevering through long hours of hand stitching and building friendships as they worked together on amazing album quilts. These women must have shared their life experiences, whether in pain or in mirth, which likely mirrored the circumstances America was experiencing as a nation.

One reason I decided to try quilting in 2005 was to "share" the experience of the women who made the treasured antique quilts. Little did I know that the quilting bug would stay and become a prominent part of my life. Throughout my quilting journey, my one burning desire has been to honor the makers of the antique quilts, many of whom are unknown, by recreating the quilts in a way that would appeal to today's quilters.

Inspired by the museum quilts presented in this book, I have reinterpreted and recreated the antique quilts with current fabrics, techniques and occasional twists of my own. I have re-sized most of the projects so present day quilters will not find them too cumbersome to complete.

My book "Recreating Antique Quilts" aims to encourage today's quilters to be inspired by the quilts and quilters of the past. By recreating the projects featured in this book, they will feel a connection to America's rich quilting history and heritage and, at the same time, be proud of their own contribution to their local quilting community and beyond.

Quilting-ly yours,

Wendy Sheppard

Calico Trail Quilt, page 10; Feathery Formation Quilt, page 64;
Priscilla's Garden Party Quilt, page 24

Calico Trail Quilt

Designed, pieced, quilted by Wendy Sheppard

Skill level: confident beginner/intermediate

Finished size approximately: 56" x 68"

Finished block size: 6" square

I love that the original quilt was constructed by using the same blocks in different orientations. I wanted to give my version of the quilt a lighter, brighter feel with updated, contemporary calico fabrics against light gray and beige background fabrics. I also gave my adapted design a final twist by adding the borders.

Split Nine Patch, Barn Raising Variation, 1930

Made by Henzeney Marie Hanson Barnes, Knowlton Township, Warren NJ

Photo by Chip Greenberg, courtesy of

The Heritage Quilt Project of New Jersey

Materials

1-3/8 yards ecru tonal print fabric

5/8 yard yellow floral print fabric

3/8 yard burgundy floral print fabric

1/4 yard blue floral print fabric

3/8 yard green floral print fabric

3/8 yard white floral print fabric

3/8 yard light green tonal texture print fabric

1-1/4 yards gray tonal texture print fabric

7/8 yard beige tonal texture print fabric

3/8 yard light purple floral print fabric

3/8 yard pink floral print fabric

3/8 yard dark purple floral print fabric

3/8 yard dark pink floral print fabric

1/4 yard dark navy tonal texture print fabric

1/4 yard light blue tonal texture print fabric

64" x 74" backing fabric

64" x 74" batting

Basic sewing supplies

Cutting Instructions

From ecru tonal print fabric, cut:

(5) 2-1/2" x 42" strips. From the strips, cut:
(80) 2-1/2" squares for blocks.

(6) 2-7/8" x 42" strips. From the strips, cut:
(80) 2-7/8" squares for blocks.

(6) 2" x 42" strips. Sew the strips together along the short end to make one continuous strip. From the strip, cut:
(2) 2" x 51-1/2" strips and
(2) 2" x 60-1/2" strips for inner border 1.

From yellow floral print fabric, cut:

(6) 2-7/8" x 42" strips. From the strips, cut:
(40) 2-7/8" squares for blocks.

From burgundy floral print fabric, cut:

(3) 2-1/2" x 42" strips. From the strips, cut:
(40) 2-1/2" squares for blocks.

From blue floral print, cut:

(2) 2-7/8" x 42" strips. From the strips, cut:
(20) 2-7/8" squares for blocks.

From green floral print fabric, cut:

(3) 2-1/2" x 42" strips. From the strips, cut:
(40) 2-1/2" squares for blocks.

From white floral print fabric, cut:

(3) 2-1/2" x 42" strips. From the strips, cut:
(40) 2-1/2" squares for blocks.

From light green tonal texture print fabric, cut:

(3) 2-1/2" x 42" strips. From the strips, cut:
(40) 2-1/2" squares for blocks.

From gray tonal texture print fabric, cut:

(7) 2-1/2" x 42" strips. Sew the strips together along the short end to make one continuous strip. From the strip, cut:
(2) 2-1/2" x 56-1/2" strips and
(2) 2-1/2" x 64-1/2" strips for outer border.

(7) 2-1/4" wide strips for binding.

From beige tonal texture print fabric, cut:

(10) 2-1/2" x 42" strips. From the strips, cut:
       (160) 2-1/2" squares for blocks.

From light purple floral print fabric, cut:

(3)   2-1/2" x 42" strips. From the strips, cut:
       (40) 2-1/2" squares for blocks.

From pink floral print fabric, cut:

(3)   2-1/2" x 42" strips. From the strips, cut:
       (40) 2-1/2" squares for blocks.

From dark purple floral print fabric, cut:

(3)   2-1/2" x 42" strips. From the strips, cut:
       (40) 2-1/2" squares for blocks.

From dark pink floral print fabric, cut:

(3)   2-1/2" x 42" strips. From the strips, cut:
       (40) 2-1/2" squares for blocks.

From light blue tonal texture print fabric, cut:

(2)   2-7/8" x 42" strips. From the strips, cut:
       (20) 2-7/8" squares for blocks.

From dark navy tonal texture print fabric, cut:

(7)   1" x 42" strips. Sew the strips together
       along the short end to make one
       continuous strip.
       From the strip, cut:
       (2) 1" x 52-1/2" strips and
       (2) 1" x 63-1/2" strips for inner border 2.

Half-square-triangle construction tip: The cutting instructions listed are exact dimensions needed for making half-square-triangle units. However, I like to make my half-square-triangle units slightly larger and then trim them to size for precision. For example, instead of cutting 2-7/8" squares to construct 2" finished half-square triangle units, I cut my squares 3" and proceed to make my half-square triangle units as normal and then trim to size.

Making the Blocks

Note: Press as you sew the pieces together.

1. Draw a diagonal line on the wrong side of a 2-7/8" ecru tonal square. Lay the marked square and a 2-7/8" yellow floral print square right sides together. Sew 1/4" on either side of the drawn line. Cut on the drawn line. Open and press to make 2 ecru tonal/yellow floral print half-square triangle units. Make 80.

Make 80

2. Referring to step 1, make 40 ecru tonal/blue floral print half-square triangle units.

Make 40

3. Lay out a 2-1/2" burgundy floral print square, a 2-1/2" pink floral print square and an ecru tonal/blue floral print half-square triangle unit, as shown. Sew the pieces together to make row 1.

Row 1

4. Lay out a 2-1/2" light purple floral print square, a 2-1/2" dark purple floral print square and a 2-1/2" beige tonal square, as shown. Sew the pieces together to make row 2.

Row 2

5. Lay out an ecru tonal/yellow floral print half-square triangle unit, a 2-1/2" beige tonal print square and a 2-1/2" ecru tonal print square, as shown. Sew the pieces together to make row 3.

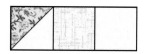

Row 3

6. Sew rows 1-3 together to complete block A. Make 20 block A.

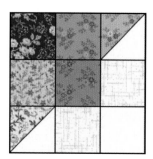

Make 20 block A

7. Referring to steps 3–6 and the block diagrams, use the remaining half-square triangle units and 2-1/2" squares to make 20 block B, 20 block C and 20 block D.

Block B

Row 1: 2-1/2" ecru tonal print square, 2-1/2" beige tonal texture print square and an ecru tonal/yellow floral print half-square triangle unit.

Row 2: 2-1/2" beige tonal texture print square, 2-1/2" light green tonal texture print square and 2-1/2" green floral print square.

Row 3: ecru tonal/blue floral print half-square triangle unit, 2-1/2" white floral print square and 2-1/2" dark pink floral print square.

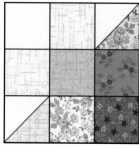

Make 20 block B

Block C

Row 1: ecru tonal/blue floral print half-square triangle unit, 2-1/2" beige tonal texture print square and 2-1/2" ecru tonal print square.

Row 2: 2-1/2" pink floral print square, 2-1/2" light green tonal texture print square and 2-1/2" beige tonal texture print square.

Row 3: 2-1/2" burgundy floral print square, 2-1/2" green floral print square and ecru tonal/yellow floral print half-square triangle unit.

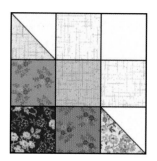

Make 20 block C

Block D

Row 1: ecru tonal/yellow floral print half-square triangle unit, 2-1/2" light purple floral print square and 2-1/2" dark pink floral print square.

Row 2: 2-1/2" beige tonal texture print square, 2-1/2" dark purple floral print square and 2-1/2" white floral print square.

Row 3: 2-1/2" ecru tonal print square, 2-1/2" beige tonal texture print square and ecru tonal/blue floral print half-square triangle unit.

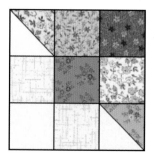

Make 20 block D

Assembling the Quilt Center

Note: Press as you sew the blocks and sections together.

Quilt center construction tip: I constructed the quilt center in sections to minimize stitching long seams. Long seams have a tendency to 'wave' during sewing.

1. Lay out the blocks in each section as shown. You will have 4 sections.

Note: Carefully note the orientation of blocks in each section.

2. Sew the blocks in each section together.

Section A
Rows 1, 3 & 5: Block A, Block B, Block A, Block B

Rows 2 & 4: Block B, Block A, Block B, Block A

Section B
Rows 1, 3 & 5: Block C, Block D, Block C, Block D

Rows 2 & 4: Block D, Block C, Block D, Block C

Section C
Rows 1, 3 & 5: Block D, Block C, Block D, Block C

Rows 2 & 4: Block C, Block D, Block C, Block D

Section D
Rows 1, 3 & 5: Block B, Block A, Block B, Block A

Rows 2 & 4: Block A, Block B, Block A, Block B,

Section A

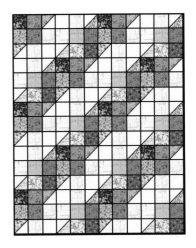

Section B

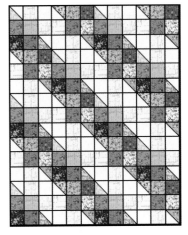

Section C

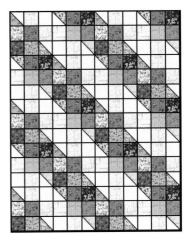

Section D

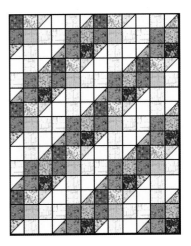

3. Sew sections A and B together to make an AB section. Sew sections C and D together to make a CD section. Sew the AB and CD sections together to complete the quilt center.

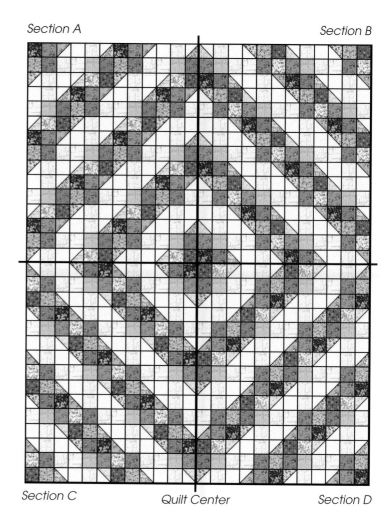

Section A   Section B

Section C   Quilt Center   Section D

Attaching the Borders

Note: Press as you sew the borders to the quilt center.

Inner Border 1
Sew the 2" x 60-1/2" ecru tonal print strips to opposite long sides of the quilt center. Sew the 2" x 51-1/2" ecru tonal print strips to the remaining sides of the quilt center.

Inner Border 2
Sew the 1" x 63-1/2" dark navy tonal texture strips to opposite long sides of the quilt center. Sew the 1" x 52-1/2" dark navy tonal texture strips to the remaining sides of the quilt center.

Outer Border
Sew the 2-1/2" x 64-1/2" gray tonal texture strips to opposite long sides of the quilt center. Sew the 2-1/2" x 56-1/2" gray tonal texture strips to the remaining sides of the quilt center to complete the quilt top.

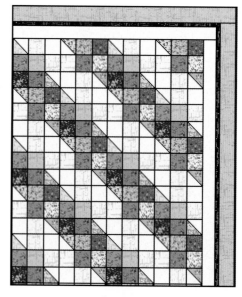

Borders

16

Finishing the Quilt

1. Lay the backing fabric, wrong side up on a flat surface. The backing fabric should be taut. Place the batting on the backing and the quilt top on the batting, right side up, to form a quilt sandwich. Baste the quilt sandwich.

2. Quilt as desired.

> **Quilting notes:** I freehand quilted dense feathers on the negative space over silk batting. The dense quilting flattened the neutral trails, letting the sparsely quilted calico trails pop and be highlighted.

3. Sew the (7) 2-1/4"-wide binding strips together along the short ends to make one continuous binding strip. Fold the piece in half lengthwise, wrong sides together, and press.

4. Square up the quilt and attach binding, hanging sleeve and label to finish.

Credits:

1. Fabrics: Quilting Treasures - Petals and Matrix collections

2. Batting: Tuscany Silk Batt by Hobbs

3. Quilting Thread: Aurifil Mako 50 Cotton

4. Museum Collection: Rutgers University Special Collections—The Heritage Quilt Project of New Jersey

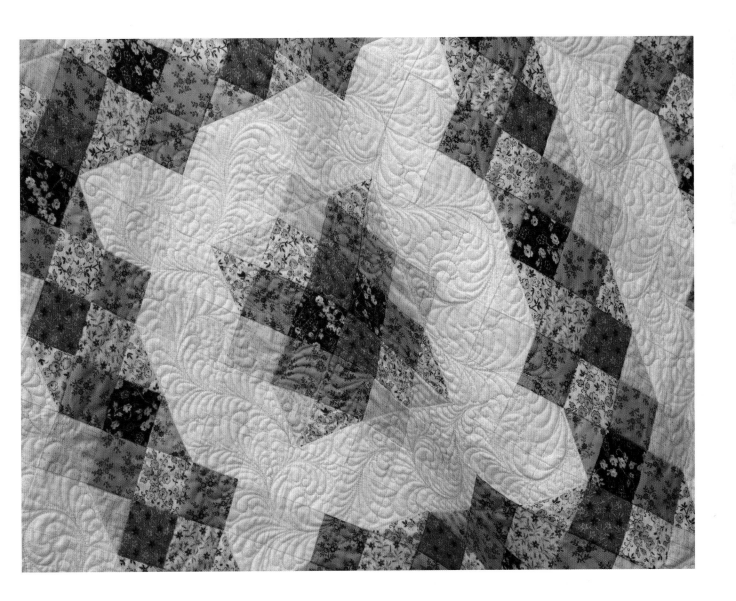

Ginkgos on Prince Street Pillow

To illustrate how the use of fabrics can change a project, I used warm-colored, triple-dyed Balis (batiks) against black background fabric for the Ginkgos on Prince Street Pillow. I also oriented the blocks in an off-centered layout. The same blocks with different fabrics and orientation produced totally different final looks.

Designed, quilted and finished by Wendy Sheppard

Skill level: confident beginner

Finished size approximately: 18" square

Finished block size: 4-1/2" square

Materials

1-3/4 yards black mottled fabric

1/8 yard orange fabric

9 fat eighths of assorted warm color batiks
Note: The featured pillow uses 2 oranges,
2 browns, 2 yellows, 1 dark mauve, 1 red
and 1 garnet.

1 – 18" square pillow form

19" x 19" batting

Basic sewing supplies

Split Nine Patch, Barn Raising Variation, 1930

Made by Henzeney Marie Hanson Barnes,
Knowlton Township, Warren NJ

Photo by Chip Greenberg, courtesy of

The Heritage Quilt Project of New Jersey

Cutting Instructions

From black mottled fabric, cut:

(2) 2" x 42" strips. From the strips, cut:
(9) 2" squares and
(9) 2" x 3 1/2" rectangles for blocks.

(1) 2-3/8" x 42" strip. From the strip, cut:
(10) 2-3/8" squares.

(2) 2-1/4" x 42" strips. From the strips, cut:
(2) 2-1/4" x 15" rectangles and
(2) 2-1/4" x 18-1/2" rectangles
for outer borders.

(1) 18-1/2" x 42" strip. From the strip, cut:
(2) 18-1/2" squares for pillow back pieces.

(1) 20" square for pillow top back piece.

From orange fabric, cut:

(2) 1" x 42" strips. From the strips, cut:
(2) 1" x 14" strips and
(2) 1" x 15" strips for inner border.

From assorted fat eighths, cut:

(20) 2" squares for block A—
5 dark mauve, 5 brown, 5 orange and 5 red.

(6) 2-3/8" squares for block A—
3 orange and 3 yellow.

(16) 2" squares for block B—
8 brown, 4 garnet and 4 yellow.

(4) 2-3/8" squares for block B—
2 orange and 2 dark mauve.

Making the Blocks

1. Draw a diagonal line on the wrong side of a 2-3/8" orange square. Lay the marked square and a 2-3/8" black mottled square right sides together. Sew 1/4" on either side of the drawn line. Cut on the drawn line. Open and press to make 2 orange/black mottled half-square triangle units. Make 10; you will only use 9.

Make 10 orange/black

2. Referring to step 1, make a total of 4 dark mauve/black mottled half-square triangle units and 6 yellow/black mottled half-square triangle units. You will use 5 of the yellow/black mottled half-square triangle units.

Make 4 dark mauve/black and 6 yellow/black

3. Lay out an orange/black mottled half-square triangle unit, a 2" dark mauve square and a 2" brown square, as shown. Sew the pieces together to make row 1.

Row 1

4. Lay out a 2" black mottled square, a 2" orange square and a 2" red square, as shown. Sew the squares together to make row 2.

Row 2

5. Lay out a 2" x 3-1/2" black mottled rectangle and a yellow/black mottled half-square triangle unit, as shown. Sew the pieces together to make row 3.

Row 3

6. Sew rows 1-3 together to complete block A. Make 5 block A.

Make 5 block A

7. Referring to steps 3-6 and the block diagram, use the remaining 2" squares and half-square triangle units make 4 block B.

Block B

Row 1 – 2" brown square, 2" garnet square and dark mauve/black mottled half-square triangle unit.

Row 2 – 2" brown square, 2" yellow square and 2" black mottled square.

Row 3 – orange/black mottled half-square triangle and a 2" x 3-1/2" black mottled rectangle.

Make 4 block B

Assembling the Pillow Center

Arrange blocks A and B in 3 rows with 3 blocks in each row.

Rows 1 and 3 – block A, block B and block A.

Row 2 – block B, block A and block B.

Sew the blocks together in rows. Sew the rows together, as shown, to make the pillow center.

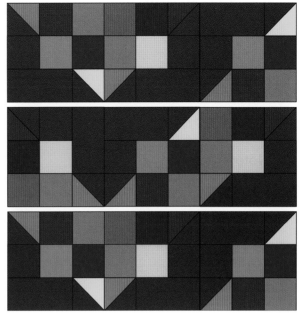

Pillow Center

Attaching the Borders

Inner border

Sew (2) 1" x 14" orange strips to opposite sides of the pillow center. Sew (2) 1" x 15" orange strips to the remaining sides of the pillow center.

Outer border

Sew (2) 2-1/4" x 15" black mottled strips to opposite sides of the pillow center. Sew (2) 2-1/4" x 18-1/2" black mottled strips to the remaining sides of the pillow center to complete pillow top.

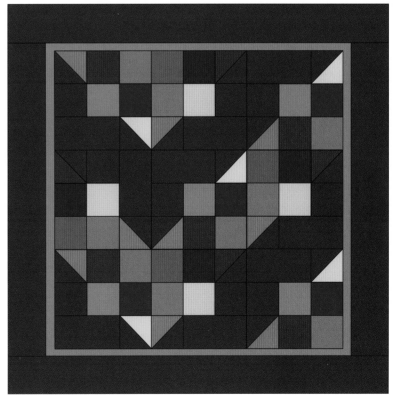

Pillow Top

Finishing the Pillow Top

1. Layer the pillow top, batting and pillow top back piece together. Baste the pieces together.

2. Quilt as desired.

Quilting Notes: I quilted my pillow top before assembling the pillow to give it a bit of a dimensional look. I treated the pillow top as a quilt, to be basted and quilted accordingly. Ginkgo leaves were quilted on the black fabric with a contrasting thread for added visual effect.

Quilting Tip: To quilt the ginkgo shapes on the pillow top, trace the motif onto a piece of freezer paper and cut it out. I auditioned placements for the cutout on the black mottled background. When I found a placement I liked, I lightly dabbed the freezer paper cutout with my iron to temporarily hold it in place on the black mottled background. Using a Clover white marker, I traced around the cutout to transfer the shape. I removed the freezer paper shape and quilted the ginkgos by following the traced outline.

3. Trim the pillow top to 18-1/2" square.

Finishing the Pillow

1. Turn under 1/4" on one edge of a black mottled 18-1/2" pillow back piece. Turn the same edge under again approximately 4". Press. Edge stitch along the outer edges of the flap to hold it in place. Repeat with the remaining 18-1/2" pillow back piece.

2. Place the quilted pillow top right side up on a flat surface. Lay the pillow back pieces on the quilted pillow top, right sides together. Adjust the pillow back pieces as needed, and trim any excess fabric from the 18-1/2" area that is not covering the pillow top.

3. Pin and stitch the pieces together around the outside edge.

Note: I used a 1/2" seam allowance for a snugger fit, but you may choose to use a 1/4" seam allowance for a looser fit.

4. Trim the corners. Finish by zigzagging the seam allowance to reduce the bulk of all the pieces stitched together.

5. Turn the pillowcase right side out. Press and insert pillow form.

Credits:

1. Fabrics: Benartex - Rainbow Bright Balis and Benartex Fantasy Island Balis
3. Batting: Hobbs Tuscany Silk Batting
4. Quilting Thread: Aurifil
5. Museum Collection: Rutgers University Special Collections—The Heritage Quilt Project of New Jersey

Ginkgo leaf motifs are full-size.

Oh, Happy Stars! Quilt, page 44

Priscilla's Garden Party Quilt

Designed, pieced, quilted by Wendy Sheppard

Specification: intermediate

Finished size approximately: 57-1/2" x 61-1/2"

The original quilt was done in a darker palette. I decided to give my adapted version the look of exploding English florals by using contemporary fabrics that have a feel of English Chintz. Fresh greens are balanced by pinks, yellows and creams in the color scheme. Large florals are contrasted by tonal floral prints as well as small floral prints. A sense of contrast and balance is how I have reinterpreted the original design.

I pay tribute to the original quilter as the unsung hero. Can you imagine hand stitching all those diamonds and triangles? To simplify the design and still retain the "spirit" of the design, I substituted the diamond strips in the quilt center with a stripe print. I also enlarged some of the diamonds and triangles to reduce the total number of units to be incorporated in my adapted version.

Bars with Diamond Sashing (1800-1849)

Courtesy of Michigan State University Museum

Materials

1-1/8 yards pink large floral print fabric

1-1/8 yards stripe print fabric
Note: Yardage given is fabric specific to featured quilt and for fussy cutting. If you are not fussy cutting the center strips you will only need 5/8 yard of fabric.

5/8 yard pink toss floral print fabric

5/8 yard yellow tonal print fabric

5/8 yard green toss floral print fabric

1/4 yard dark green tonal print fabric

3/8 yard cream large floral print fabric

1 yard cream tonal print fabric

1/4 yard light green tonal print fabric

3/8 yard lavender tonal print fabric

1 yard cream toss floral print fabric

3/4 yard dark pink tonal print fabric

63" x 67" backing fabric

63" x 67" batting

Basic sewing supplies

Cutting Instructions

From pink large floral print fabric, cut:

(3)   5-1/2" x 42" strips. From the strips, cut:
(3) 5-1/2" x 35-1/2" rectangles.

(5)   3-1/4" x 42" strips.
Sew the strips together along the short ends to make one continuous strip. From the strip, cut: (2) 3-1/4" x 45-1/2" strips and (2) 3-1/4" x 47" strips for inner border 3.

From stripe print fabric, cut lengthwise:
35-1/2"-long piece of fabric.
Focusing on the narrow stripe print, fussy cut:
(2) 2" x 34-1/2" strips and
(6) 2" x 35-1/2" strips.
Four of these strips will be used for inner border 1.

Note: The fabric used has 8 repeats of narrow stripe strips. If you are not using a fabric identical to the one shown, don't worry about the repeats. Just make sure the correct number of strips are cut.

* If you are not fussy cutting, cut:

(8)   2" x 42" strips. From the strips, cut:
(2) 2" x 34-1/2" and
(6) 2" x 35-1/2" strips. Four of these strips will be used for inner border 1.

From pink toss floral print fabric, cut:

(10) diamonds using the D template on page 35 for side inner border 2.

(12) diamonds using the H template on page 37 for top/bottom inner border 2.

(2)   diamonds using the K template on page 38 for corner blocks.

(12) triangles using the F template on page 36 for outer border.

From yellow tonal print fabric, cut:

(10) diamonds using the D template on page 35 for side inner border 2.

(6) diamonds using the H template on page 37 for top/bottom inner border 2.

(2) diamonds using the K template on page 38 for corner blocks.

(12) triangles using the F template on page 36 for outer border.

From green toss floral print fabric, cut:

(4) diamonds using the K template on page 38 for corner blocks.

(10) diamonds using the D template on page 35 for side inner border 2.

(6) diamonds using the H template on page 37 for top/bottom inner border 2.

(12) triangles using the F template on page 36 for outer border.

From dark green tonal print fabric, cut:

(12) triangles using the F template on page 36 for outer border.

From cream large floral print fabric, cut:

(2) 5-1/2" x 42" strips. From the strips, cut: (2) 5-1/2" x 35-1/2" strips.

From cream tonal print fabric, cut:

(40) triangles using the A template on page 35 for side inner border 2.

(40) triangles using the B template on page 35 for side inner border 2.

(40) triangles using the C template on page 35 for side inner border 2.

(68) triangles using the I template on page 37 for top/bottom inner border 2.

(68) triangles using the J template on page 37 for top/bottom inner border 2.

(8) triangles using the L template on page 38 for corner blocks.

(8) triangles using the M template on page 38 for corner blocks.

(8) triangles using the N template on page 38 for corner blocks.

(6) 1-1/2" x 42" strips.
Sew the strips together along the short ends to make one continuous strip.
From the strip, cut:
(2) 1-1/2" x 49" strips and
(2) 1-1/2" x 51" strips for inner border 4.

From light green tonal print fabric, cut:

(4) diamonds using the H template on page 37 for top/bottom inner border 2.

From lavender tonal print fabric, cut:

(10) diamonds using the D template on page 35 for side inner border 2.

(6) diamonds using the H template on page 37 for top/bottom inner border 2.

From cream toss floral print fabric, cut:

(58) triangles using the E template on page 36 for outer border.

(58) triangles using the G template on page 36 for outer border.

(4) 5" squares for outer border.

From dark pink tonal print fabric, cut:

(10) triangles using the F template on page 36 for outer border.

(7) 2-1/4"-wide binding strips.

Accurate Template Piecing

When piecing, I like all my points to match, or at least appear to match. I have found the following technique extremely helpful in achieving accurate piecing when using templates.

1. Print a copy of the templates needed for the project. If a copier is not available, carefully trace the templates onto plain paper using the outer edge of the 1/4" seam allowance line as a guide.

2. Using a scissors, cut out the template leaving 1/8" – 1/4" of paper around the seam allowance. Do not cut directly on the seam allowance line.

3. Attach a few pieces of double-sided tape onto the wrong side of the paper template.

4. Place the paper template, right side up, on the right side of the pressed fabric. The tape will temporarily hold the paper template in place while you cut out the fabric piece.

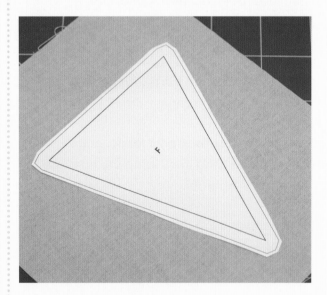

Note: I cut my fabric by referencing the edge of the shape, which means I do not go by the seam allowance line on the template when I cut.

5. Line up the 1/4" line on the ruler on top of the template's dark line. It is safer to trust the 1/4" on the ruler than the 1/4" printed on the paper. While the 1/4" seam allowance printed on the paper is most likely accurate, it is better to be safe than have to recut the template.

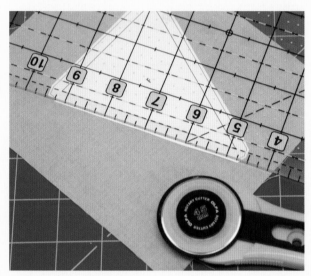

6. Cut the fabric shape all the way around repositioning the ruler as necessary.

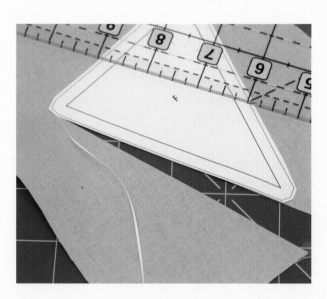

Assembling the Quilt Center

Note: Press as you sew the strips together.

1. Lay out (4) 2" x 35-1/2" stripe print strips, (2) 5-1/2" x 35-1/2" cream large floral print strips and (3) 5-1/2" x 35-1/2" pink large floral print strips as shown.

2. Sew the strips together to complete the quilt center.

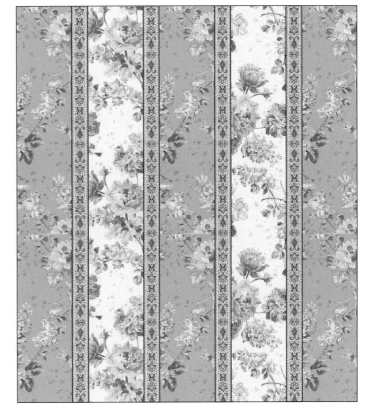

Quilt Center

Attaching the Borders

Note: Press as you sew the borders to the quilt center.

Inner border 1

1. Sew (2) 2" x 35-1/2" stripe print strips to opposite long sides of the quilt center.

2. Sew (2) 2" x 34-1/2" stripe print strips to the remaining sides of the quilt center.

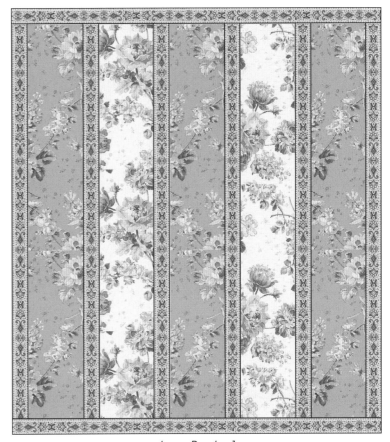

Inner Border 1

29

Inner border 2

Making the blocks

Note: Steps 1-3: blocks for side inner border #2 strips
Steps 4-5: blocks for corner blocks in inner border #2
Steps 8-10: blocks for top/bottom inner border #2 strips

1. Lay out 1 lavender tonal print D diamond, 1 green toss floral D diamond, 2 cream tonal print B triangles and 2 cream tonal print C triangles in diagonal rows as shown.

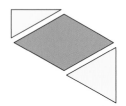 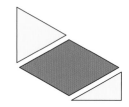

2. Sew the pieces together in diagonal rows. Press. Sew the diagonal rows together. Press.

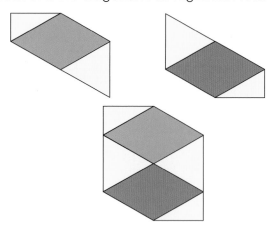

3. Sew a cream tonal print A triangle to the remaining corners to complete a lavender/green double diamond block. Make a total of 10 lavender tonal/green toss floral and a total of 10 yellow tonal/pink toss floral double diamond blocks.

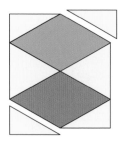 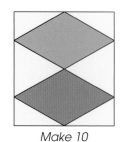 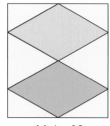

Make 10   *Make 10*

4. Lay out 1 yellow tonal print K diamond, 1 green toss floral K diamond, 2 cream tonal print L triangles and 2 cream tonal print M triangles in diagonal rows as shown.

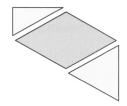 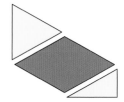

5. Sew the pieces together in diagonal rows. Press. Sew the diagonal rows together. Press.

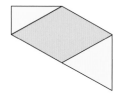 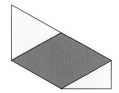

6. Sew a cream tonal print N triangle to the remaining corners to complete a yellow/light green toss floral corner block. Make a total of 2 yellow tonal/light green corner blocks.

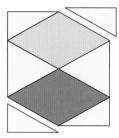 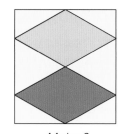

Make 2

7. Referring to steps 4-6, make 2 pink toss floral/green toss floral corner blocks.

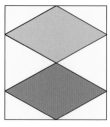

Make 2

8. Lay out 1 yellow tonal print H diamond, 2 cream tonal print I triangles and 2 cream tonal print J triangles as shown.

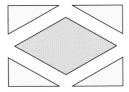

9. Sew the I triangles to opposite sides of the H diamond. Press. Sew the J triangles to the remaining sides of the H diamond. Press to make a yellow tonal diamond block. Make a total of 6 yellow tonal diamond blocks.

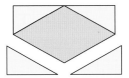 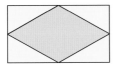

Make 6

10. Referring to steps 8-9, make 12 pink toss floral diamond blocks, 6 lavender tonal diamond blocks, 6 green toss floral diamond blocks and 4 light green tonal diamond blocks.

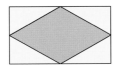

Make 12

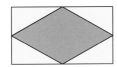

Make 6

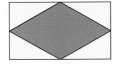

Make 6

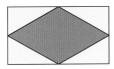

Make 4

11. Lay out 5 lavender tonal/green toss double diamond blocks and 5 yellow tonal/pink toss floral double diamond blocks, alternating blocks in the row. Sew the blocks together to make 1 side inner border 2. Press. Repeat to make an additional side inner border 2.

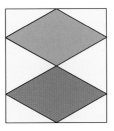

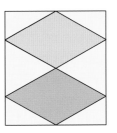

31

12. Sew side inner border 2 to the left and right sides of the quilt center, as shown.

13. Referring to the diagram, arrange the single diamond blocks in 2 rows with 17 blocks in each row. Sew the blocks together in rows. Press.

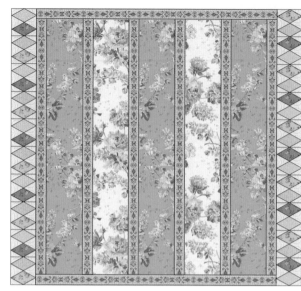

Inner Border 2

14. Sew a corner block to opposite ends of the single diamond rows. Sew the rows to the top and bottom of the quilt center. Press.

Inner Border 2

Inner border 3

Sew (2) 3-1/4" x 45-1/2" pink large floral print strips to the opposite long sides of the quilt center.
Sew (2) 3-1/4" x 47" pink large floral print strips to the remaining sides of the quilt center.

Inner border 4

Sew (2) 1-1/2" x 51" cream tonal print strips to the opposite long sides of the quilt center.
Sew (2) 1-1/2" x 49" cream tonal print strips to the remaining opposite sides of the quilt center.

Inner Borders 3 & 4

Outer border

Making the blocks

1. Lay out 1 dark green tonal print F triangle, 1 cream toss floral print E triangle and 1 cream toss floral print G triangle as shown.

2. Sew the E and G triangles to opposite sides of the F triangle. Press to make a dark green outer block. Make a total of 12 dark green tonal outer blocks.

Make 12

3. Referring to steps 1-2, make 12 green toss floral outer blocks, 12 yellow tonal outer blocks, 12 pink toss floral outer blocks and 10 dark pink tonal outer blocks.

 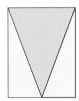

Make 12   *Make 12*

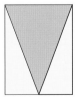 

Make 12   *Make 10*

4. Lay out 3 dark green tonal, 3 green toss floral, 3 yellow tonal, 3 pink toss floral and 3 dark pink tonal outer blocks in a row as shown. Sew the blocks together to make 1 side outer border. Press. Repeat to make an additional side outer border.

5. Sew side outer borders to the left and right sides of the quilt center, as shown.

6. Lay out 3 dark green tonal, 3 green toss floral, 3 yellow tonal, 3 pink toss floral and 2 dark pink tonal outer blocks in a row as shown. Sew the blocks together to make 1 top/bottom outer border. Press. Repeat to make an additional top/bottom outer border.

7. Sew a 5" cream toss floral print square to opposite ends of the top/bottom outer border. Sew the borders to the top and bottom of the quilt center. Press to complete the quilt top.

Finishing the Quilt

1. Lay the backing fabric, wrong side up on a flat surface. The backing fabric should be taut. Layer batting and quilt top, right side up, on top of backing to form a quilt sandwich. Baste the quilt sandwich.

2. Quilt as desired.

Quilting Notes: Feathers are quilted all over the quilt to add the "fancy" feel of a garden tea party.

3. Sew the (7) 2-1/4"-wide binding strips together along the short ends to make one continuous binding strip. Fold the piece in half lengthwise, wrong sides together, and press.

4. Square up the quilt and attach binding, hanging sleeve and label to finish.

Credits:
1. Fabrics: Benartex - Rosemont Gazebo
2. Batting: Tuscany Silk Batt by Hobbs
3. Quilting Thread: Aurifil Mako 50 Cotton
4. Museum Collection: Michigan State University

Outer Border

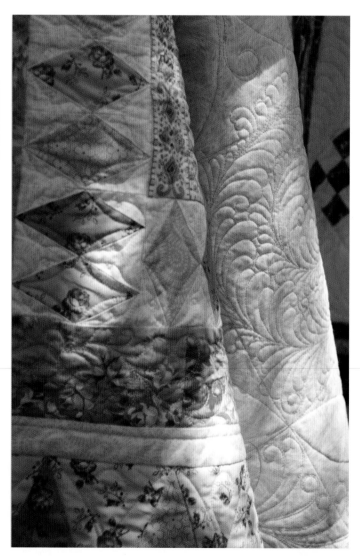

34

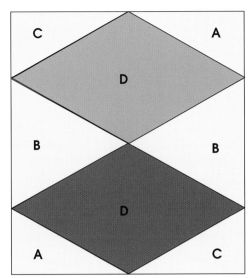

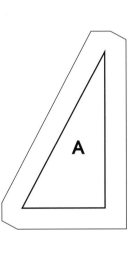

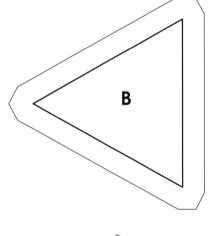

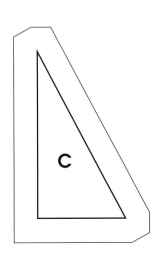

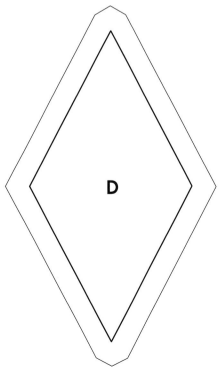

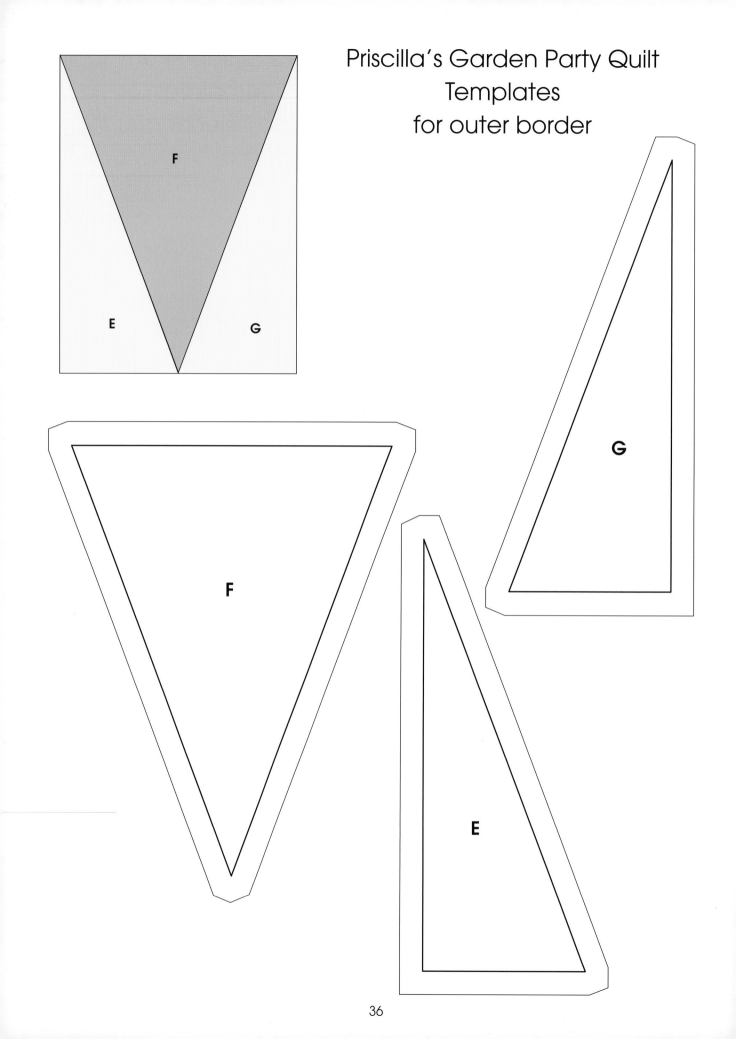

Priscilla's Garden Party Quilt
Templates
for outer border

F

E   G

F

G

E

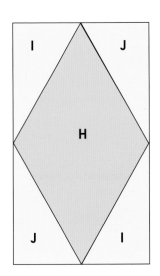

Priscilla's Garden Party Quilt
Templates
for top/bottom inner border #2

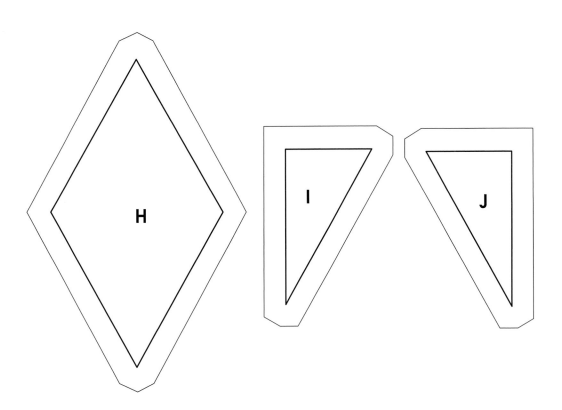

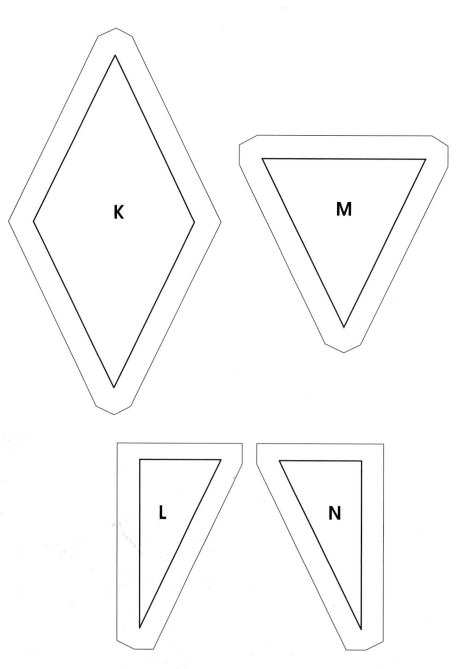

Priscilla's Garden Party Quilt
Templates
for inner border #2
corner blocks

38

Priscilla's Garden Party Quilt, page 24; Garden Lattice Quilt, page 40

Garden Lattice Quilt

Designed, pieced, quilted by Wendy Sheppard

Specification: beginner

Finished size approximately: 57-1/2" x 61-1/2"

Materials

1 yard cream large floral print fabric

1/2 yard yellow floral print fabric

5/8 yard cream floral cluster print fabric

2 yards stripe print fabric
Note: Yardage given is fabric specific to featured quilt and for fussy cutting. If you are not fussy cutting the center strips you will only need 1-3/8 yards of fabric.

3/4 yard olive tonal print fabric

3/8 yard cream tonal print fabric

63" x 67" backing fabric

63" x 67" batting

Basic sewing supplies

Bars with Diamond Sashing (1800-1849)
Courtesy of Michigan State University Museum

Cutting Instructions

Cutting tip: The quilt center stripe print strips should be cut to length specified in cutting instructions before piecing. Trimming the strips to size after piecing will compromise accuracy and distort the final size of the quilt center.

From cream large floral print fabric, cut:
(5) 5-1/2" x 42" strips. From the strips, cut:
(5) 5-1/2" x 35-1/2" rectangles.

From yellow floral print fabric, cut:
(4) 3-1/2" x 42" strips. From the strips, cut:
(2) 3-1/2" x 38-1/2" strips and
(2) 3-1/2" x 40-1/2" strips for inner border 2.

From cream floral cluster print fabric, cut:
(5) 3-1/4" x 42" strips. Sew the strips together along the short ends to make one continuous strip.
From the strip, cut:
(2) 3-1/4" x 45-1/2" strips and (2) 3-1/4" x 47" strips for inner border 4.

From stripe print fabric, cut lengthwise:
35-1/2"-long piece of fabric.
Focusing on the narrow stripe print, fussy cut:
(2) 2" x 34-1/2" and
(6) 2" x 35-1/2" strips. Four of these strips will be used for inner border 1.

Note: The fabric used has 8 repeats of narrow stripe strips. If you are not using a fabric identical to the one shown, don't worry about the repeats. Just make sure the correct number of strips are cut.

* If you are not fussy cutting, cut:
(8) 2" x 42" strips. From the strips, cut:
(2) 2" x 34-1/2" strips and
(6) 2" x 35-1/2" strips. Four of these strips will be used for inner border 1.

From stripe print fabric, cut:

(6) 5" x 42" strips. Sew the strips together along the short ends to make one continuous strip. From the strip, cut:
(2) 5" x 53" and
(2) 5" x 58" strips for outer border.

From olive tonal print fabric, cut:

(5) 1" x 42" strips. Sew the strips together along the short ends to make one continuous strip. From the strip, cut:
(2) 1" x 41-1/2" and
(2) 1" x 44-1/2" strips for inner border 3.

(7) 2-1/4"-wide binding strips.

From cream tonal print fabric, cut:

(6) 1-1/2" x 42" strips. Sew the strips together along the short ends to make one continuous strip. From the strip, cut:
(2) 1-1/2" x 49" strips and
(2) 1-1/2" x 51" strips for inner border 5.

Assembling the Quilt Center

Note: Press as you sew the strips together.

1. Lay out (4) 2" x 35-1/2" stripe print strips and (5) 5-1/2" x 35-1/2" cream large floral print strips as shown.

2. Sew the strips together to complete the quilt center.

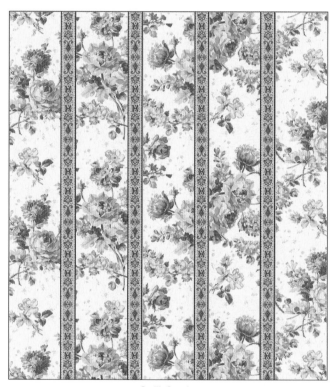

Quilt Center

Attaching the Borders

Note: Press as you sew the borders to the quilt center.

Inner border 1

Sew (2) 2" x 35-1/2" stripe print strips to opposite long sides of the quilt center. Sew (2) 2" x 34-1/2" stripe print strips to the remaining sides of the quilt center.

Inner border 2

Sew (2) 3-1/2" x 38-1/2" yellow floral print strips to opposite long sides of the quilt center. Sew (2) 3-1/2" x 40-1/2" yellow floral print strips to the remaining sides of the quilt center.

Inner border 3

Sew (2) 1" x 44-1/2" olive tonal print strips to opposite long sides of the quilt center.

Sew (2) 1" x 41-1/2" olive tonal print strips to the remaining sides of the quilt center.

Inner border 4

Sew (2) 3-1/4" x 45-1/2" cream floral cluster print strips to opposite long sides of the quilt center.

Sew (2) 3-1/4" x 47" cream floral cluster print strips to the remaining sides of the quilt center.

Inner border 5

Sew (2) 1-1/2" x 51" cream tonal print strips to opposite long sides of the quilt center.

Sew (2) 1-1/2" x 49" cream tonal print strips to the remaining sides of the quilt center.

Outer border

Sew (2) 5" x 53" stripe print strips to opposite long sides of the quilt center. Sew (2) 5" x 58" stripe print strips to the remaining sides of the quilt center to complete the quilt top.

Borders

Finishing the Quilt

1. Lay the backing fabric, wrong side up on a flat surface. The backing fabric should be taut. Layer batting and quilt top, right side up, on top of backing to form a quilt sandwich. Baste the quilt sandwich.

2. Quilt as desired.

Quilting notes: I used a mixture of free-motion quilted swirls, vines and feathers.

3. Sew the (7) 2-1/4"-wide binding strips together along the short ends to make one continuous binding strip. Fold the piece in half lengthwise, wrong sides together, and press.

4. Square up the quilt and attach binding, hanging sleeve and label to finish.

Credits:

1. Fabrics: Benartex - Rosemont Gazebo
2. Batting: Tuscany Silk Batt by Hobbs
3. Quilting Thread: Aurifil Mako 50 Cotton
4. Museum Collection: Michigan State University

Oh, Happy Stars! Quilt

Designed, pieced, quilted by Wendy Sheppard

Specification: confident intermediate/advanced

Finished size approximately: 45" square

Finished block size: 5" square

The scrappy feel of the original quilt attracted me. I brightened up my adapted version with contemporary bright tonal print fabrics for a bright and happy scrappy look. The five patch blocks are colored in such a way that the dark plum squares give the illusion of shadows in between blocks. I like the clean look of the white outer border for quilting. A stylized bird appliqué in the top right corner of the quilt presents a bit of unpredicted bling. Traditional appliqué quilts seem to abide by an unwritten rule—appliqué pieces must stay within the "designated appliqué" areas. I let my appliqué swirls spill over onto the pieced blocks to add visual interest to the overall design.

Double Irish Chain with Sawtooth Star, 1840-1850

Made by Mrs. Frank Miles, Watchung , Somerset, NJ

Photo by Chip Greenberg, courtesy of
The Heritage Quilt Project of New Jersey

Materials

1-1/2 yards solid white fabric

5/8 yard plum tonal print fabric

5/8 yard beige tonal print fabric

1/2 yard green tonal print fabric

1/2 yard dark pink tonal print fabric

3/8 yard orange tonal print fabric

1/2 yard blue tonal print fabric

3/8 yard light pink tonal print fabric

3/8 yard gray tonal print fabric

3/8 yard lime tonal print fabric

1/4 yard solid taupe fabric

Assorted 1/8-1/4 yard fabrics in shades of blue, green and pink for appliqué

1/2 yard light blue tonal print fabric for binding

50" x 50" backing fabric

50" x 50" batting

Basic sewing supplies

Supplies for appliqué method of choice

Cutting Instructions

Note: Any 1-1/2" x 42" strips remaining after cutting will be used for piecing the 25-patch blocks.

From solid white fabric, cut:

(2) 1-1/4" x 42" strips. From the strips, cut:
(48) 1-1/4" squares for star blocks.

(1) 2-3/4" x 42" strip. From the strip, cut:
(12) 2-3/4" squares for star blocks.

(12) 1-1/2" x 42" strips.
From 4 strips, cut:
(48) 1-1/2" x 3-1/2" rectangles for star blocks.
From 2 strips, cut:
(31) 1-1/2" squares for 25-patch and pieced border blocks.
From 3 strips, cut:
(6) 1-1/2" x 21" strips for 25-patch and pieced border blocks.
From 2 strips, cut:
(24) 1-1/2" x 2-1/2" rectangles for pieced border blocks.

(2) 3-1/2" x 42" strips. From the strips, cut:
(12) 3-1/2" x 5-1/2" rectangles for pieced border blocks.

(3) 5-1/2" x 42" strips.
From the strips, cut:
(12) 5-1/2" squares
(4) 5-1/2" x 10-1/2" rectangles for outer border blocks.

From plum tonal print fabric, cut:
(12) 1-1/2" x 42" strips for 25-patch blocks.

From beige tonal print fabric, cut:
(2) 1-1/4" x 42" strips. From the strips, cut:
(48) 1-1/4" squares for star blocks.

(8) 1-1/2" x 42" strips.
From 4 strips, cut:
(48) 1-1/2" x 3-1/2" rectangles for star blocks.
From 4 strips, cut:
(7) 1-1/2" x 21" strips for 25-patch and pieced border blocks.

(1)   2-3/4" x 42" strip. From the strip, cut:
      (12) 2-3/4" squares for star blocks.

From green tonal print fabric, cut:
(2)   1-5/8" x 42" strips.
      From each strip, cut:
      (16) 1-5/8" squares for white and
          beige star blocks.

(5)   1-1/2" x 42" strips.
      From the strips, cut:
      (16) 1-1/2" squares for white and
          beige star blocks.
      (2) 1-1/2" x 21" strips for 25-patch and
          pieced border blocks.
      (2) 1-1/2" squares for pieced border blocks.

(4) 2" squares for white and beige star blocks.

From dark pink tonal print fabric, cut:
(2)   1-5/8" x 42" strips.
      From the strips, cut:
      (20) 1-5/8" squares for white and
          beige star blocks.

(6)   1-1/2" x 42" strips.
      From the strips, cut:
      (20) 1-1/2" squares for white and
          beige star blocks.
      (1) 1-1/2" x 21" strip for 25-patch and
          pieced border blocks.
      (4) 1-1/2" squares for pieced border blocks.

(5) 2" squares for white and beige star blocks.

From orange tonal print fabric, cut:
(2)   1-5/8" x 42" strips.
      From the strips, cut:
      (12) 1-5/8" squares for white and
          beige star blocks.

(3)   1-1/2" x 42" strips.
      From the strips, cut:
      (12) 1-1/2" squares for white and
          beige star blocks.

      (2) 1-1/2" x 21" strips for 25-patch and
          pieced border blocks.
      (1) 1-1/2" square for pieced border blocks.

(3) 2" squares for white and beige star blocks.

From blue tonal print fabric, cut:
(2)   1-5/8" x 42" strips.
      From the strips, cut:
      (16) 1-5/8" squares for white and
          beige star blocks.

(4)   1-1/2" x 42" strips.
      From the strips, cut:
      (16) 1-1/2" squares for white and
          beige star blocks.
      (2) 1-1/2" x 21" strips for 25-patch and
          pieced border blocks.
      (1) 1-1/2" square for pieced border blocks.

(4) 2" squares for white and beige star blocks.

From light pink tonal print fabric, cut:
(2)   1-5/8" x 42" strips.
      From the strips, cut:
      (12) 1-5/8" squares for white and
          beige star blocks.

(3) 1-1/2" x 42" strips.
      From the strips, cut:
      (12) 1-1/2" squares for white and
          beige star blocks.
      (2) 1-1/2" x 21" strips for 25-patch and
          pieced border blocks.
      (1) 1-1/2" square for pieced border blocks.

(3) 2" squares for white and beige star blocks.

From gray tonal print fabric, cut:
(2)   1-5/8" x 42" strips.
      From the strips, cut:
      (12) 1-5/8" squares for white and
          beige star blocks.

(3)　1-1/2" x 42" strips.

From the strips, cut:

(12) 1-1/2" squares for white and
beige star blocks.

(2) 1-1/2" x 21" strips for 25-patch and
pieced border blocks.

(2) 1-1/2" squares for pieced border blocks.

(3) 2" squares for white and beige star blocks.

From lime tonal print fabric, cut:

(2)　1-5/8" x 42" strips.

From the strips, cut:

(8) 1-5/8" squares for white and
beige star blocks.

(3)　1-1/2" x 42" strips.

From the strips, cut:

(8) 1-1/2" squares for white and
beige star blocks.

(2) 1-1/2" x 21" strips for 25-patch and
pieced border blocks.

(1) 1-1/2" square.

(2) 2" squares for white and beige star blocks.

From solid taupe fabric, cut:

(3)　1-1/2" x 42" strips for 25-patch blocks.

From light blue tonal print fabric, cut:

(5)　2-1/4"-wide binding strips.

From the assorted 1/8-1/4 yard fabrics in shades of blue, green and pink, cut:

Appliqué shapes using the templates on
pages 54-57.

Making the 25-Patch Blocks

Construction notes: You may wish to construct the quilt block-by-block and row-by-row as the project progresses in order to keep everything straight.

Note: Read through Piecing Small Squares Accurately on page 74 to piece the block segments without any 'wonkiness'.

1.　Sew a 1-1/2" x 42" solid taupe strip and a 1-1/2" x 42" plum tonal strip together along one long edge to make a strip set. Make 2 strip sets. Cut the strip sets into 1-1/2" segments. You will need 32 taupe/plum segments.

2.　Referring to step 1, use the 1-1/2" x 42" strips to make the following strip sets. Cut the strip sets into 1-1/2" segments.

Note: Any extra segments will be used to construct the pieced border blocks.

(1) Plum tonal/lime tonal strip set to make
14 plum/lime segments.

(1) Plum tonal/green tonal strip set to make
28 plum/green segments.

(1) Plum tonal/gray tonal strip set to make
20 plum/gray segments.

(1) Plum tonal/light pink tonal strip set to make
22 plum/light pink segments.

(1) Plum tonal/orange tonal strip set to make
22 plum/orange segments.

(2) Plum tonal/blue tonal strip sets to make
30 plum/blue segments.

(2) Plum tonal/dark pink tonal strip sets to make 32 plum/dark pink segments.

(1) Solid taupe/solid white strip set to make 16 taupe/white segments.

(1) Solid white/dark pink tonal strip set to make 14 white/dark pink segments.

3. Referring to step 1, use the 1-1/2" x 21" strips to make the following strip sets. Cut the strip sets into 1-1/2" segments.

(1) Solid white/green tonal strip set to make 9 white/green segments.

(1) Solid white/orange tonal strip set to make 9 white/orange segments.

(1) Solid white/blue tonal strip set to make 10 white/blue segments.

(1) Solid white/light pink tonal strip set to make 9 white/light pink segments.

(1) Solid white/gray tonal strip set to make 7 white/gray segments.

(1) Solid white/lime tonal strip set to make 6 white/lime segments.

(1) Beige tonal/dark pink tonal strip set to make 10 beige/dark pink segments.

(1) Beige tonal/green tonal strip set to make 7 beige/green segments.

(1) Beige tonal/light pink tonal strip set to make 4 beige/light pink segments.

(1) Beige tonal/lime tonal strip set to make 3 beige/lime segments.

(1) Beige tonal/gray tonal strip set to make 7 beige/gray segments.

(1) Beige tonal/blue tonal strip set to make 7 beige/blue segments.

(1) Beige tonal/orange tonal strip set to make 4 beige/orange segments.

4. Lay out 4 plum/taupe, 2 taupe/white, 2 plum/dark pink, 2 plum/green, 1 white/dark pink and 1 beige/green segments and 1 solid white 1-1/2" square as shown.

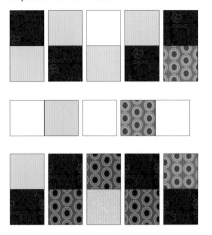

5. Sew the segments together in rows.

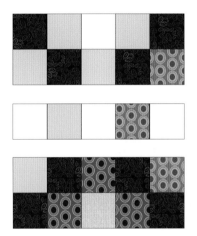

6. Sew the rows together to complete the 25-patch block

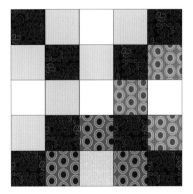

7. Referring to the quilt center diagram on page 51 for color placement, make the remaining 25-patch blocks for a total of (25) 25-patch blocks.

Making the Star Blocks

1. Draw a diagonal line on the wrong side of all the 1-5/8" dark pink tonal squares.

2. With right sides together, lay the marked squares on opposite corners of a 2-3/4" solid white square. Make sure the drawn lines on the smaller squares are aligned. Stitch a scant 1/4" on both sides of the drawn line.

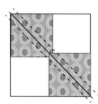

3. Cut on the drawn line to make 2 units. Open and press the seams toward the dark pink tonal squares.

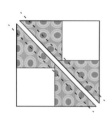

4. Lay a marked 1-5/8" dark pink tonal square on the corner of one of the units from step 3, right sides together. Stitch a scant 1/4" on both sides of the drawn line. Cut on the drawn line. Press open to make 2 flying geese units.

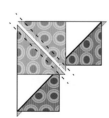

Make 2

5. Repeat with the remaining unit to make a total of 4 flying geese units.

6. Lay a flying geese unit on one side of a 2" dark pink tonal square, right sides together. Make sure the point of the flying geese unit is aligned with the raw edge of the square. Sew the pieces together and press open. Repeat with another flying geese unit on the opposite side of the square to make the center row.

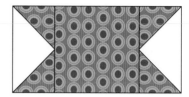

7. Sew 1-1/4" solid white squares to opposite sides of a flying geese unit to make a row. Repeat to make a total of 2 rows.

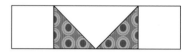

8. Sew the rows together to complete the star block center.

9. Sew 1-1/2" x 3-1/2" solid white rectangles to opposite sides of the star block center.

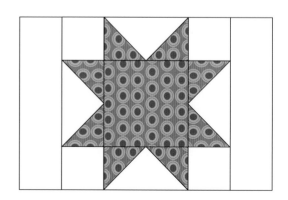

10. Sew 1-1/2" dark pink tonal squares to opposite sides of a 1-1/2" x 3-1/2" solid white rectangle to make a row. Repeat to make a total of 2 rows. Sew the rows to the remaining sides of the star block center to complete a white/dark pink Star block. Make a total of 2 white/dark pink Star blocks.

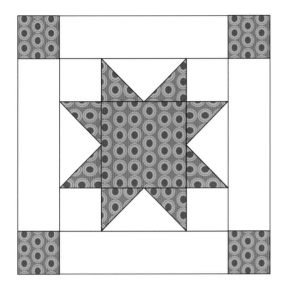

11. Referring to steps 1-10, make Star blocks in the following colorways:

(2) white/green tonal

(1) white/gray tonal

(2) white/orange tonal

(2) white/blue tonal

(1) white/lime tonal

(2) white/light pink tonal

(2) beige tonal/green tonal

(1) beige tonal/light pink tonal

(1) beige tonal/orange tonal

(1) beige tonal/lime tonal

(3) beige tonal/dark pink tonal

(2) beige tonal/gray tonal

(2) beige tonal/blue tonal

Quilt Center Assembly

1. Referring to the Row Assembly Diagrams and the quilt photo on page 44, lay out the 25-Patch blocks and Star blocks in 7 rows in the color/block placement shown.

2. Sew the rows together to complete the quilt center.

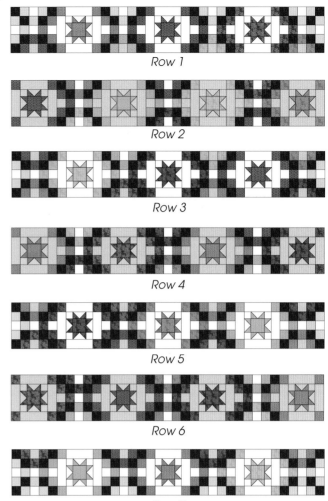

Row 1

Row 2

Row 3

Row 4

Row 5

Row 6

Row 7
Row Assembly Diagrams

Quilt Center Diagram

Making the Pieced Border Blocks

1. Lay out 2 white/dark pink segments and a 1-1/2" white square. Sew the pieces together in a row as shown.

2. Lay out (2) 1-1/2" x 2-1/2" solid white rectangles and a 1-1/2" dark pink tonal square. Sew the pieces together in a row as shown.

3. Sew the rows from steps 1-2 and a 3-1/2" x 5-1/2" solid white rectangle together to make a white/dark pink Pieced Border block. Make a total of 2 white/dark pink Pieced Border blocks.

Make 2

4. Referring to steps 1-3 and the Quilt Top Assembly Diagram for color placement, make the remaining (10) Pieced Border blocks for a total of (12) Pieced Border blocks.

Quilt Top Assembly

1. Referring to the Quilt Top Assembly Diagram and the quilt photo on page 44, lay out the Quilt Center, Pieced Border blocks, 5-1/2" solid white squares and 5-1/2" x 10-1/2" solid white rectangles as shown.

2. Sew the pieces on the left side of the quilt center together in a row. Repeat with the pieces on the right side of the quilt center.

3. Sew the side rows to the quilt center.

4. Sew the pieces on the top of the quilt center together in a row. Repeat with the pieces on the bottom of the quilt center.

5. Sew the top/bottom rows to the quilt center to complete the quilt top.

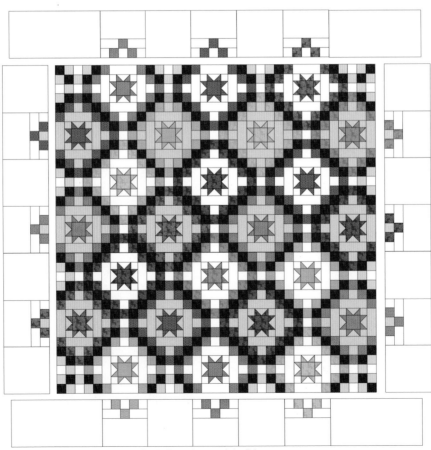

Quilt Top Assembly Diagram

Adding the Appliqué

1. Prepare the appliqué pieces using your favorite method. Fusible appliqué was used on the Oh, Happy Stars! quilt. Referring to the photograph on page 44, arrange the prepared appliqué pieces on the quilt top.

2. Sew pieces in place using a favorite appliqué stitch. The appliqué pieces on Oh, Happy Stars! were stitched with small blanket stitches. Refer to Appliqué Stitching Tips on page 83 for helpful hints on stitching the appliqué shapes.

Finishing the Quilt

1. Lay the backing fabric, wrong side up on a flat surface. The backing fabric should be taut. Layer batting and quilt top, right side up, on top of backing to form a quilt sandwich. Baste the quilt sandwich.

2. Quilt as desired.

> **Quilting Notes:** Textured swirl quilting was used in the quilt center. The dense quilting in the white border—a mixture of informal feathers and pebbles—gives a secondary design to the overall look of quilt.

3. Sew the (5) 2-1/4"-wide light blue tonal binding strips together along the short ends to make one continuous binding strip. Fold the piece in half lengthwise, wrong sides together, and press.

4. Square up the quilt and attach the binding, hanging sleeve and label to finish.

Credits:

1. Fabrics: Art Gallery Fabrics - Pure Elements, Nature Elements, Oval Elements, Floral Elements

2. Batting: Tuscany Silk Batt by Hobbs

3. Quilting Thread: Aurifil Mako 50 Cotton

4. Museum Collection: Rutgers University Special Collections—The Heritage Quilt Project of New Jersey

Oh, Happy Stars! Quilt Templates

*These templates have been reversed
for use with fusible appliqué*

C

A

- - - - *Underlay Lines*

B

E

D

Oh, Happy Stars! Quilt Templates

*These templates have been reversed
for use with fusible appliqué*

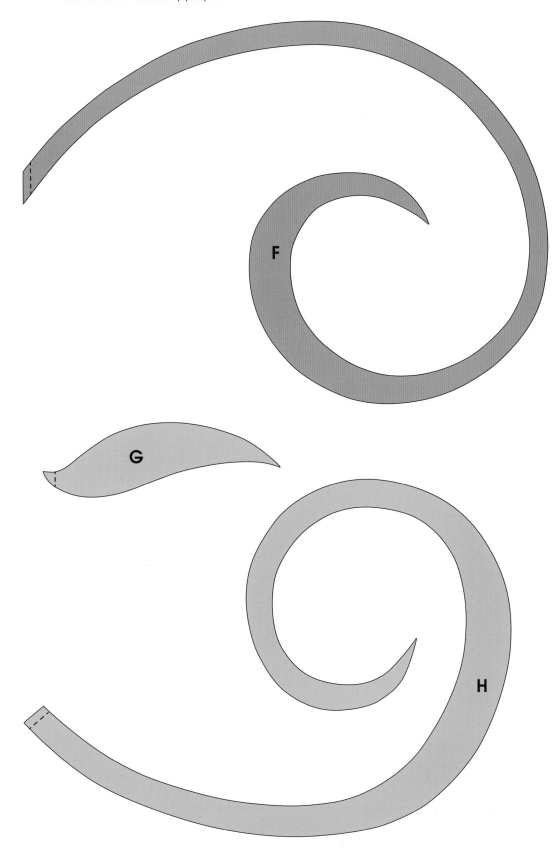

Oh, Happy Stars! Quilt Templates

These templates have been reversed for use with fusible appliqué

- - - - *Underlay Lines*

K

J

I

L

Match Dotted Lines

M

N

Match Dotted Lines

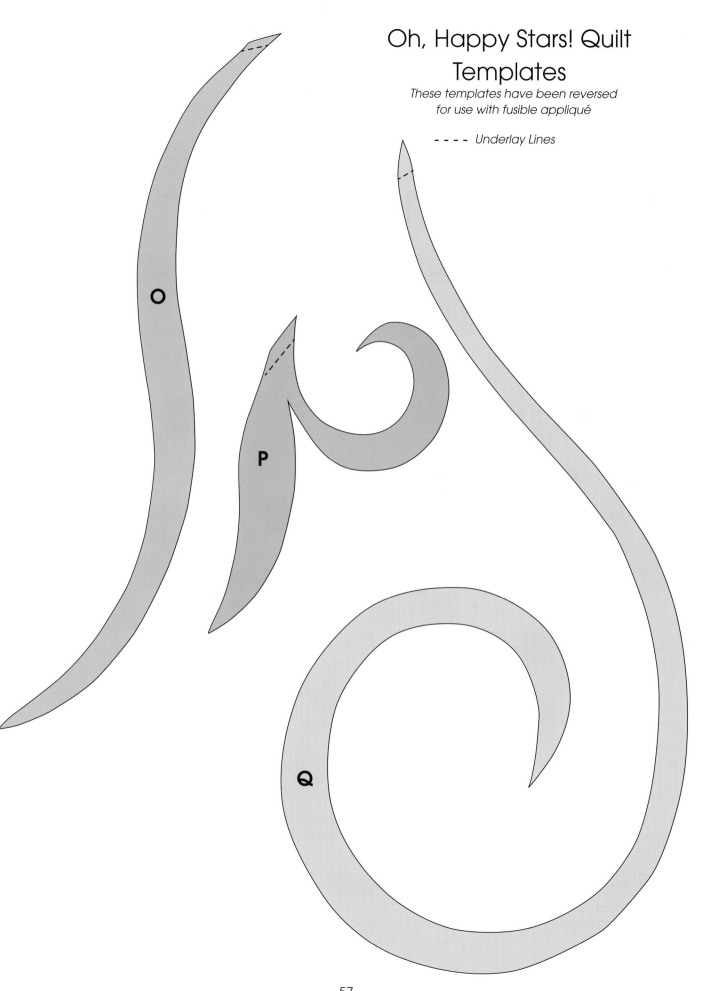

O

P

Q

Stars & Snowflakes Table Topper

Designed, pieced, quilted by Wendy Sheppard

Specification: beginner

Finished size approximately: 35-1/2" square

Finished block size: 10" square

This quick to complete project uses Christmas theme fabrics and colorway for a seasonal project. I added the blue to the traditional Christmas green and red colorway to give a little pop to the overall color scheme.

Double Irish Chain with Sawtooth Star, 1840-1850

Made by Mrs. Frank Miles, Watchung , Somerset, NJ

Photo by Chip Greenberg, courtesy of
The Heritage Quilt Project of New Jersey

Materials

1/4 yard light green dotted print fabric

5/8 yard star print fabric

1/2 yard red tonal print fabric

3/8 yard gold dotted print fabric

1/4 yard neutral tonal fabric

1/4 yard neutral print fabric

1/4 yard blue print fabric

3/8 yard green print fabric

3/8 yard light green print fabric

3/4 yard pink print fabric

40" x 40" backing fabric

40" x 40" batting

Basic sewing supplies

Cutting Instructions

From light green dotted print fabric, cut:
(1)   2-1/2" x 42" strip, From the strip, cut:
       (16) 2-1/2" squares for 25-patch blocks.

From star print fabric, cut:
(2)   2-1/2" x 42" strips, From the strips, cut:
       (20) 2-1/2" squares for 25-patch blocks.

(3)   2" x 42" strips. From the strips, cut:
       (16) 2" squares and
       (16) 2" x 3-1/2" rectangles for star blocks.

(3)   2-1/2" x 42" strips. From the strips, cut:
       (16) 2-1/2" x 6-1/2" rectangles for star blocks.

From red tonal print fabric, cut:
(2)   2-1/2" x 42" strips. From the strips, cut:
       (18) 2-1/2" squares for 25-patch blocks.

(1)   2" x 42" strip. From the strip, cut:
       (16) 2" squares for star blocks.

(1)   3-1/2" x 42" strip. From the strip, cut:
(2)   3-1/2" squares and
      (8) 2-1/2" squares for star blocks.

From gold dotted print fabric, cut:
(1)   2-1/2" x 42" strip. From the strip, cut:
      (13) 2-1/2" squares for 25-patch blocks.

(4)   1" x 42" strips. From the strips, cut:
      (2) 1" x 30-1/2" strips and
      (2) 1" x 31-1/2" strips for inner border 1.

From neutral tonal fabric, cut:
(4)   1" x 42" strips. From the strips, cut:
      (2) 1" x 31-1/2" and
      (2) 1" x 32-1/2" strips for inner border 2.

From neutral print fabric, cut:
(2)   2-1/2" x 42" strips. From the strips, cut:
      (24) 2-1/2" squares for 25-patch blocks.

From blue print fabric, cut:
(2)   2-1/2" x 42" strips. From the strips, cut:
      (16) 2-1/2" squares for 25-patch blocks.

From green print fabric, cut:
(1)   2-1/2" x 42" strip. From the strip, cut:
      (9) 2-1/2" squares for 25-patch blocks.

(1)   3-1/2" x 42" strip. From the strip, cut:
      (1) 3-1/2" square, (4) 2-1/2" squares and
      (8) 2" squares for star blocks.

From light green print fabric, cut:
(1)   2-1/2" x 42" strip. From the strip, cut:
      (9) 2-1/2" squares for 25-patch blocks.

(1)   3-1/2" x 42" strip. From the strip, cut:
      (1) 3-1/2" square,
      (4) 2-1/2" squares and
      (8) 2" squares for star blocks.

From pink print fabric, cut:
(4)   2-1/4" x 42" strips. From the strips, cut:
      (2) 2-1/4" x 32-1/2" strips and
      (2) 2-1/4" x 36" strips for outer border.

(4)   2-1/4"-wide binding strips.

Making the 25-Patch Blocks

Note: Read through Piecing Small Squares Accurately on page 74 to piece the block segments without any 'wonkiness'.

Referring to the diagrams and color placement, lay out the 2-1/2" squares in 5 horizontal rows with 5 squares in each row. Sew the squares together in rows. Sew the rows together to complete the 25-patch blocks. Make 1 block in each colorway for a total of (5) 25-patch blocks.

1. Rows 1 & 5 – gold dotted print, red tonal print, star print, red tonal print, gold dotted print

   Rows 2 & 4 – green print, light green dotted print, red tonal print, light green dotted print, light green print

   Row 3 – star print, green print, gold dotted print, light green print, star print

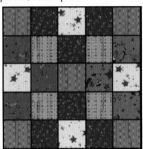

2. Row 1 – light green dotted print, neutral print, star print, blue print, neutral print

   Row 2 – neutral print, gold dotted print, blue print, neutral print, red tonal print

   Row 3 – star print, blue print, light green dotted print, red tonal print, star print

   Row 4 – blue print, neutral print, green print, gold dotted print, red tonal print

   Row 5 – neutral print, green print, star print, green print, light green dotted print

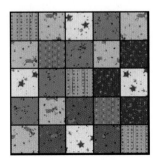

3. Row 1 – neutral print, green print, star print, green print, light green dotted print

Row 2 – blue print, neutral print, green print, gold dotted print, red tonal print

Row 3 – star print, blue print, light green dotted print, red tonal print, star print

Row 4 – neutral print, gold dotted print, blue print, neutral print, red tonal print

Row 5 – light green dotted print, neutral print, star print, blue print, neutral print

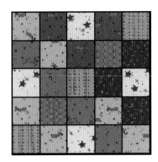

4. Row 1 – neutral print, blue print, star print, neutral print, light green dotted print

Row 2 – red tonal print, neutral print, blue print, gold dotted print, neutral print

Row 3 – star print, red tonal print, light green dotted print, blue print, star print

Row 4 – red tonal print, gold dotted print, light green print, neutral print, blue print

Row 5 – light green dotted print, light green print, star print, light green print, neutral print

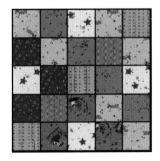

5. Row 1 – light green dotted print, light green print, star print, light green print, neutral print

Row 2 – red tonal print, gold dotted print, light green print, neutral print, blue print

Row 3 – star print, red tonal print, light green dotted print, blue print, star print

Row 4 – red tonal print, neutral print, blue print, gold dotted print, neutral print

Row 5 – neutral print, blue print, star print, neutral print, light green dotted print

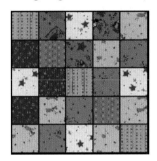

Making the Star Blocks

1. Draw a diagonal line on the wrong side of (2) 2" red tonal print squares. Lay one of the marked squares on one corner of a 2" x 3-1/2" star print rectangle, right sides together. Sew on the drawn line. Trim 1/4" from the sewn line. Press open to reveal red tonal print corner triangle. Repeat with the remaining marked square on the opposite corner of the rectangle. Press to complete 1 flying geese unit, Make a total of 4 flying geese units.

Make 4

2. Lay a flying geese unit on one side of a 3-1/2" red tonal square, right sides together. Make sure the point of the flying geese unit is aligned with the raw edge of the square. Sew the pieces together and press open. Repeat with another flying geese unit on the opposite side of the square.

Make 2

3. Sew (2) 2" star print squares to opposite sides of the remaining flying geese units.

Make 2

4. Sew the pieces made in steps 2-3 together to complete the star block center, as shown.

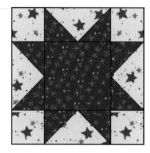

5. Sew (2) 2-1/2" x 6-1/2" star print rectangles to opposite sides of the star block center.

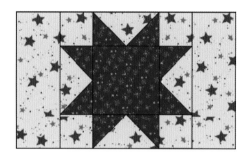

6. Sew (2) 2-1/2" red tonal print squares to opposite sides of a 2-1/2" x 6-1/2" star print rectangle, Repeat to make a total of 2.

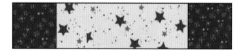

Make 2

7. Sew the pieces made in steps 5-6 together to complete the red tonal star block. Make 2 red tonal star blocks.

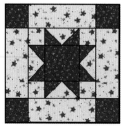

Make 2

8. Referring to steps 1-7, make 1 green print star block and 1 light green print star block. You will have a total of 4 star blocks.

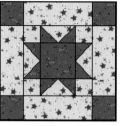

Make 1   *Make 1*

Assembling the Table Topper Center

1. Lay out the (5) 25-patch blocks and 4 star blocks in 3 horizontal rows as shown. Carefully watch the placement and orientation of the 25-patch blocks.

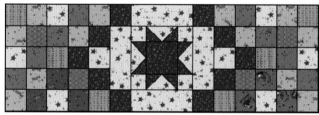

Row 1

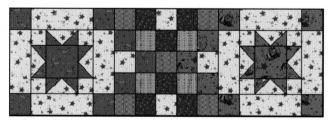

Row 2

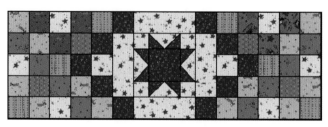

Row 3

2. Sew the blocks together in rows. Sew the rows together to complete the table topper center.

Table Topper Center

Attaching the Borders

Note: Press as you sew the borders to the table topper center.

Inner border 1
Sew (2) 1" x 30-1/2" gold dotted print strips to opposite sides of the table topper center. Sew (2) 1" x 31-1/2" gold dotted print strips to the remaining sides of the table topper center.

Inner border 2
Sew (2) 1" x 31-1/2" neutral tonal strips to opposite sides of the table topper center. Sew (2) 1" x 32-1/2" neutral tonal strips to the remaining sides of the table topper center.

Outer border
Sew (2) 2-1/4" x 32-1/2" pink print strips to opposite sides of the table topper center. Sew (2) 2-1/4" x 36" pink print strips to the remaining sides of the table topper center to complete the table topper top.

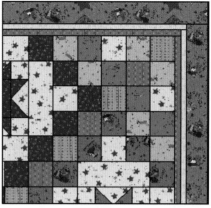

Borders

Finishing the Table Topper

1. Lay the backing fabric, wrong side up on a flat surface. The backing fabric should be taut. Layer batting and quilt top, right side up, on top of backing to form a quilt sandwich. Baste the quilt sandwich.

2. Quilt as desired.

Quilting Notes: Quilting was kept relatively simple for this table topper with cross-hatching in the 25-patch blocks and simple swirls and curls on the star blocks. Snowflakes were free-motion quilted in the outer border to add to the whimsical feel of the table topper.

3. Sew the (4) 2-1/4"-wide binding strips together along the short ends to make one continuous binding strip. Fold the piece in half lengthwise, wrong sides together, and press.

4. Square up the table topper and attach binding, hanging sleeve and label to finish.

Credits:
1. Fabrics: RJR Fabrics - Starry Night
2. Batting: Tuscany Silk Batt by Hobbs
3. Quilting Thread: Aurifil Mako 50 Cotton
4. Museum Collection: Rutgers University Special Collections—The Heritage Quilt Project of New Jersey

Feathery Formation Quilt

Designed, pieced, quilted by Wendy Sheppard

Specification: intermediate

Finished size approximately: 58" square

Finished block size: 9" square

The original red and white split nine patch blocks captured my attention with the look of uniformity. I decided to make my adapted version smaller and with a variety of colors. The mix of colors gives the quilt a lighter, more informal feel. Quilting off center feather wreaths in the negative space enhanced my contemporary take on the overall appearance of the quilt.

Building Blocks, Hannah (Anna) Russell Harmon, Circa 1890

Courtesy Illinois State Museum

Museum Photographer: Doug Carr

Materials

1/4 yard each purple nest print fabric, orange leaf print fabric, aqua geometric print fabric, light blue leaf print fabric and dark blue leaf print fabric

1 yard of blue bird focal print fabric

3/8 yard pink geometric print fabric

2-5/8 yards solid cream fabric

1/2 yard brown berry print fabric

1/2 yard dark brown berry print fabric

62" x 62" backing fabric

62" x 62" batting

Basic sewing supplies

Cutting Instructions

Cutting notes: Exact measurements are given for cutting the border strips, but due to the on-point setting you may wish to measure and cut the border strips after the quilt center is complete.

From each purple nest print, orange leaf print, aqua geometric print, light blue leaf print, dark blue leaf print fabrics, cut:

(2)   1-1/2" x 42" strips. From 1 strip, cut:
(1) 1-1/2" x 14" strip. Set the remaining strip and leftover pieces aside.

Note: If you don't wish to strip piece the blocks, you will need to cut (40) 1-1/2" squares from each fabric.

(1)   3-1/2" x 42" strip. From the strip, cut:
(8) 1-1/2" x 3-1/2" rectangles and
(2) 3-1/2" squares.

From blue bird focal print fabric, cut:

(4)   1-1/2" x 42" strips. From 1 strip, cut:
(1) 1-1/2" x 26" strip.
Set the remaining strips and leftover pieces aside.

Note: If you don't wish to strip piece the blocks, you will need to cut (80) 1-1/2" squares.

(1)   3-1/2" x 42" strip. From the strip, cut:
(16) 1-1/2" x 3-1/2" rectangles and
(4) 3-1/2" squares.

(6)   2-1/2" x 42" strips. Sew the strips together along the short end to make one continuous strip. From the strip, cut:
(2) 2-1/2" x 54-1/2" strips and
(2) 2-1/2" x 58-1/2" strips for outer border.

From pink geometric print fabric, cut:

(6)   1-1/4" x 42" strips. Sew the strips together along the short end to make one continuous strip. From the strip, cut:
(2) 1-1/4" x 53" strips and
(2) 1-1/4" x 54-1/2" strips for inner border 2.

From solid cream fabric, cut:

(21)   1-1/2" x 42" strips. From the strips, cut:
(2) 1-1/2" x 26" strips,
(12) 1-1/2" x 14" strips and
(128) 1-1/2" x 3-1/2" rectangles.
Set the remaining strips and leftover pieces aside.

Note: If you don't wish to strip piece the blocks, you will need to cut (256) 1-1/2" squares.

(3)   9-1/2" x 42" strips. From the strips, cut:
(9) 9-1/2" setting squares.

(2)   14" x 42" strips. From the strips, cut:
(3) 14" squares. Cut the squares in half twice on the diagonal to make 12 side setting triangles.

(2)   7-1/4" squares.
Cut the squares in half once on the diagonal to make 4 corner setting triangles.

From brown berry print fabric, cut:

(2)   1-1/2" x 42" strips. From 1 strip, cut:
(1) 1-1/2" x 14" strip.

Note: If you don't wish to strip piece the blocks, you will need to cut (40) 1-1/2" squares.

(2) 3-1/2" squares.

(6) 1-1/4" x 42" strips. Sew the strips together along the short end to make one continuous strip. From the strip, cut:
(2) 1-1/4" x 51-1/2" strips and
(2) 1-1/4" x 53" strips for inner border 1.

From dark brown berry print fabric, cut:

(6) 2-1/4" -wide binding strips.

Making the Blocks

Note: Read through Piecing Small Squares Accurately on page 74 to piece the block segments without any 'wonkiness'.

1. Sew 1-1/2" x 14" solid cream strips to opposite long sides of a 1-1/2" x 14" orange leaf strip to make a strip set.

2. Cut the strip set into (8) 1-1/2" orange leaf B segments.

Cut 8

3. Referring to steps 1-2, use the remaining 1-1/2" x 14" solid cream strips and the 1-1/2" x 14" purple nest, aqua geometric, light blue leaf and dark blue leaf print strips to make (8) 1-1/2" B segments in each colorway.

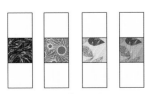

Cut 8 each

4. In the same manner, sew 1-1/2" x 26" solid cream strips to opposite long sides of a 1-1/2" x 26" blue bird focal print strip to make a strip set. Cut the strip set into (16) 1-1/2" B segments.

Cut 16

5. Sew 1-1/2" x 42" blue bird focal print strips to opposite long sides of a 1-1/2" x 42" solid cream strip to make a strip set.

6. Cut the strip set into (28) 1-1/2" A segments. Use enough of the remaining blue bird focal print strip pieces and solid cream strip pieces to make (4) 1-1/2" A segments for a total of (32) blue bird focal print A segments.

Cut 32

7. Sew the remaining 1-1/2" -wide orange leaf strips to opposite long sides of a 1-1/2" -wide solid cream strip to make a strip set. You will need a strip set that is 28" long.

8. Cut the strip set into (16) 1-1/2" orange leaf A segments.

Cut 16

9. Referring to steps 7-8, use the remaining 1-1/2"-wide solid cream strips and 1-1/2"-wide purple nest, aqua geometric, light blue leaf and dark blue leaf print fabrics to make (16) 1-1/2" A segments in each colorway.

Make 16 each

10. Lay out 2 orange leaf A segments and 1 orange leaf B segment as shown. Sew the segments together to make 1 orange leaf 9-patch unit. Make a total of 4 orange leaf 9-patch units.

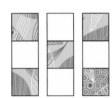

Make 4

11. Lay out (2) 1-1/2" x 3-1/2" solid cream rectangles and (1) 1-1/2" x 3-1/2" orange leaf rectangle. Sew the rectangles together to make a stripe unit. Make a total of 4 stripe units.

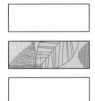

Make 4

12. Lay out (4) 9-patch units, 4 stripe units and (1) 3-1/2" orange leaf square as shown. Sew the pieces together in rows.

13. Sew rows together to complete 1 orange leaf block. Make a total of 2 orange leaf blocks.

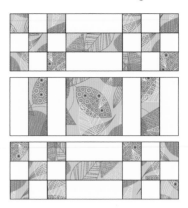

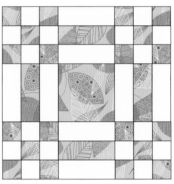

Make 2

14. Referring to steps 10-13, make 2 purple nest print blocks, 2 aqua geometric print blocks, 2 light blue leaf print blocks, 2 dark blue leaf print blocks, 2 brown berry print blocks and 4 blue bird focal print blocks.

Assembling the Quilt Center

1. Lay out the blocks and setting triangles in diagonal rows as shown.

Note: Carefully note the placement of the blocks within each row.

Rows 1 & 7 - solid cream side setting triangle, purple nest print block, solid cream side setting triangle.

Rows 2 & 6 - solid cream side setting triangle, dark blue leaf print block, solid cream setting square, blue bird focal print block, solid cream side setting triangle.
Note: Blocks are placed differently in each row.

Rows 3 & 5 - solid cream side setting triangle, blue bird focal print block, solid cream setting square, aqua geometric print block, solid cream setting square, light blue leaf print block, solid cream side setting triangle.
Note: Blocks are placed differently in each row.

Row 4 - brown berry print block, solid cream setting square, orange leaf print block, cream solid setting square, brown berry print block, solid cream setting block, orange leaf print block.

2. Sew the pieces together in diagonal rows.

3. Sew the diagonal rows together. Sew a solid cream corner setting triangle to each of the corners to complete quilt center. The quilt center length should measure approximately 51-1/2" long from raw edge to raw edge.

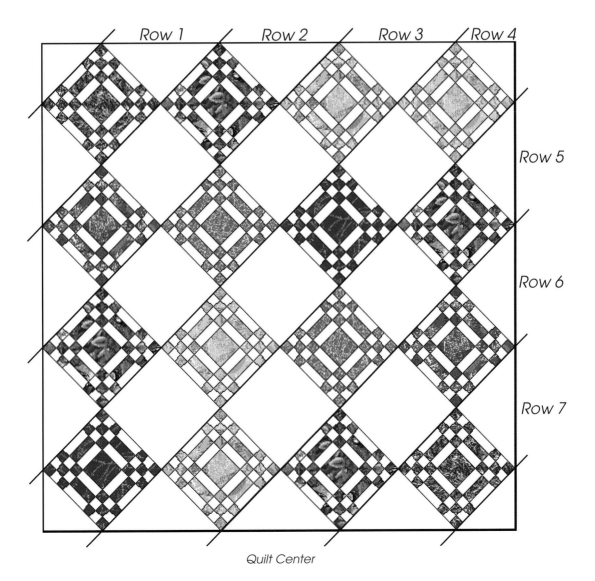

Quilt Center

Attaching the Borders

Inner border 1

Sew the 1-1/4" x 51-1/2" brown berry print strips to opposite sides of the quilt center. Sew the 1-1/4" x 53" brown berry print strips to the remaining sides of the quilt center.

Inner border 2

Sew the 1-1/4" x 53" pink geometric print strips to opposite sides of the quilt center. Sew the 1-1/4" x 54-1/2" pink geometric print strips to the remaining sides of the quilt center.

Outer border

Sew the 2-1/2" x 54-1/2" blue bird focal print strips to opposite sides of the quilt center. Sew the 2-1/2" x 58-1/2" blue bird focal print strips to the remaining sides of the quilt center to complete the quilt top.

Borders

Finishing the Quilt

1. Lay the backing fabric, wrong side up on a flat surface. The backing fabric should be taut. Layer batting and runner top, right side up, on top of backing to form a quilt sandwich. Baste the quilt sandwich.

2. Quilt as desired. Refer to page 71 for my off-centered feather wreath quilting design.

Quilting Notes: I added a contemporary twist to the traditional feather wreaths that were often quilted on setting squares of historical quilts. My feather wreaths are quilted off-center and concentric. Using a thread a few shades darker than the cream added a bit of contrast.

3. Sew the (6) 2-1/4" -wide binding strips together along the short ends to make one continuous binding strip. Fold the piece in half lengthwise, wrong sides together, and press.

4. Square up the quilt and attach the binding, hanging sleeve and label to finish.

Credits:

1. Fabrics: RJR Fabrics - Flutter by Alex Anderson
2. Batting: Tuscany Silk Batt by Hobbs
3. Quilting Thread: Aurifil Mako 50 Cotton
4. Museum Collection: Illinois State Museum

Off-centered Feather Wreath Quilting Design

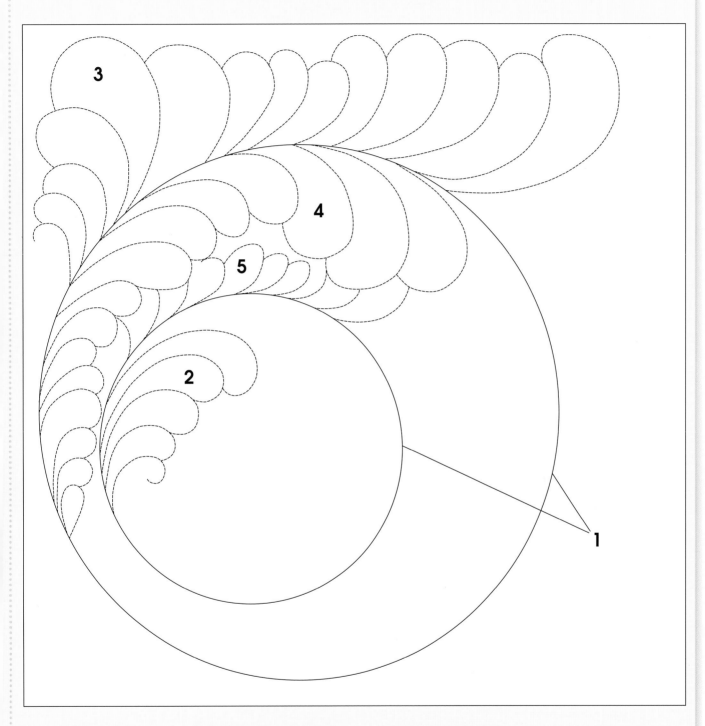

1. Lightly draw the two circles.

2. Quilt feathers in innermost ring.

3. Quilt feathers in outermost ring.

4. Mirror feathers in outermost ring. These feathers are often quilted in such a way that they appear to overlap.

5. Mirror feathers in innermost ring.

Patches & Crosses
Table Runner

Designed, pieced, quilted by Wendy Sheppard

Specification: intermediate

Finished size approximately: 50" x 21-3/4"

Finished block size: 9" square

Materials

1/2 yard light gray geometric print fabric

1/4 yard brown tonal print fabric

3/8 yard pink geometric print fabric

3/8 yard dark gray leaf print fabric

3/8 yard orange leaf print fabric

3/8 yard cream solid fabric

1/2 yard leaf/bird focal print fabric

3/8 yard dark brown berry print fabric

26" x 54" backing fabric

26" x 54" batting

Basic sewing supplies

Building Blocks, Hannah (Anna) Russell Harmon, Circa 1890

Courtesy Illinois State Museum

Museum Photographer: Doug Carr

Cutting Instructions:

Cutting notes: Measurements are given for cutting the border strips, but due to the on-point setting you may wish to measure and cut the border strips after the table runner center is complete.

From light gray geometric print fabric, cut:

(3) 1-1/2" x 42" strips. From the strips, cut:
(72) 1-1/2" squares.

(2) 3-1/2" x 42" strips. From the strips, cut:
(2) 3-1/2" squares and
(24) 1-1/2" x 3-1/2" rectangles.

From brown tonal print fabric, cut:

(2) 1-1/2" x 42" strips. From the strips, cut:
(48) 1-1/2" squares.

(1) 3-1/2" x 42" strip. From the strip, cut:
(4) 3-1/2" squares.

From pink geometric print fabric, cut:

(4) 1-1/2" x 42" strips. From the strips, cut:
(32) 1-1/2" squares and
(16) 1-1/2" x 3-1/2" rectangles.
Set the remaining fabric aside.

(3) 1-1/2" sashing squares.

(4) 1" x 42" strips. From 1 strip, cut:
(2) 1" x 16-1/4" strips for inner border 2.
Sew the remaining 3 strips together along the short end to make one continuous strip.
From the strip, cut:
(2) 1" x 45-1/2" strips for inner border 2.

From dark gray leaf print fabric, cut:

(4) 3" x 42" strips. From 1 strip, cut:
(2) 3" x 17-1/4" strips for outer border.
Sew the remaining 3 strips together along the short ends to make one continuous strip.
From the strip, cut:
(2) 3" x 50-1/2" strips for outer border.

Piecing Small Squares Accurately

The idea of piecing small squares into larger units seems like a no-brainer. After all, it can't be that hard to sew a bunch of squares together. Unfortunately, I have found that oftentimes after piecing, my pieced square is nothing close to square. I end up having to trim to try to square up the block, but find there's really nothing to trim because the whole unit is wonky.

I have found the following method helps keep the wonkiness out of my pieced blocks. The example uses 1-1/2" strips and is sewn with a scant 1/4" seam.

1. Sew (2) 1-1/2" strips together along one long edge. Do not press the strips open. You may notice that the strips have a 'wave' where they have been sewn together.

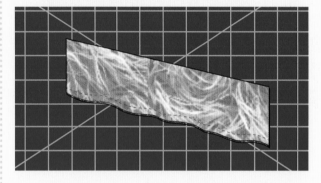

2. Carefully press the sewn strips on both sides without pulling or stretching the fabric. The waviness should disappear.

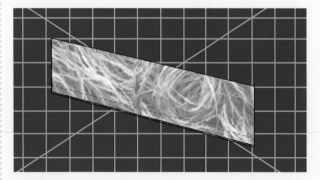

3. Keeping the strips layered together cut units at 1-1/2" intervals.

4. Finger press the pieced units open. Do not iron as the heat from the iron could distort the weave at this point. The distortion might not be much if you were making larger squares, but it could make a difference when piecing 1-1/2" squares.

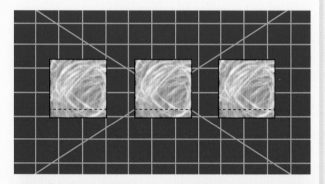

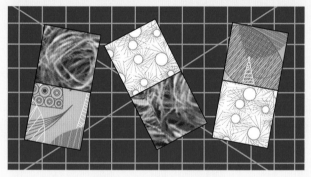

5. If you are using this method to make 9-patch blocks, sew a 1-1/2" square to the pieced unit in step 4. Finger press to make the first row for the 9-patch block. Make the number of rows or units needed for your block.

6. Sew the rows or units together to make the block.

7. Square up the block. You should only have a thread or two to trim away. At this point, you can gently press and set the block with an iron.

From orange leaf print fabric, cut:

(5)   1-1/2" x 42" strips. From the strips, cut:
        (64) 1-1/2" squares and
        (32) 1-1/2" x 3-1/2" rectangles.

From cream solid fabric, cut:

(5)   1-1/2" x 42" strips. From the strips, cut:
        (4) 1-1/2" x 9-1/2" strips and
        (8) 1-1/2" x 12" strips for sashing rectangles.

(4)   1-1/4" x 42" strips. From 1 strip, cut:
        (2) 1-1/4" x 14-3/4" strips for inner border 1.
        Sew the remaining 3 strips together along the
        short end to make one continuous strip.
        From the strip, cut:
        (2) 1-1/4" x 44-1/2" strips for inner border 1.

From leaf/bird focal print fabric, cut:

(1)   14" square. Cut the square in half twice on
        the diagonal to make 4 side setting triangles.

From dark brown berry print fabric, cut:

(4) 2 1/4" -wide binding strips.

Making the Blocks

*Note: The 9-patch blocks are constructed with
individual squares sewn into segments. You can strip
piece the segments if you prefer, using my tip for
Piecing Small Squares Accurately on page 74.*

1. Referring to the diagram, lay out (3) 1-1/2"
   brown tonal print squares, (4) 1-1/2" orange leaf
   print squares and (2) light gray geometric print
   squares as shown. Sew the squares together
   to make a 9-patch unit. Make a total of (4)
   9-patch units.

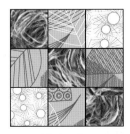

Make 4

2. Lay out (2) 1-1/2" x 3-1/2" orange leaf
   rectangles and (1) 1-1/2" x 3-1/2" light gray
   geometric print rectangle. Sew the rectangles
   together to make a stripe unit. Make a total of
   4 stripe units.

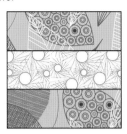

Make 4

3. Lay out (4) 9-patch units, 4 stripe units and (1)
   3-1/2" brown tonal square as shown. Sew the
   pieces together in rows.

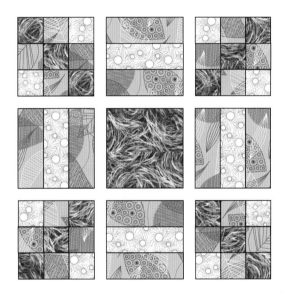

4. Sew the rows together to complete 1 orange/
   brown 9-patch block. Make a total of 4
   orange/brown 9-patch blocks.

Make 4

5. Referring to steps 1-4 and using the pink geometric print 1-1/2" squares, 1-1/2" x 3-1/2" rectangles, light gray geometric print 1-1/2" squares and 1-1/2" x 3-1/2" rectangles, make 2 pink/gray 9-patch blocks.

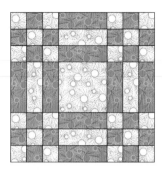

Make 2

Making the Sashing Rows

1. Lay out (2) 1-1/2" x 12" cream solid sashing rectangles and (1) 1-1/2" pink geometric print sashing square as shown.

2. Sew the pieces together to make a sashing row. Make a total of 3 sashing rows.

Assembling the Runner Center

1. Lay out 1 orange/brown 9-patch block, 1 leaf/bird focal print setting triangle and (1) 1-1/2" x 12" cream solid sashing rectangle in a diagonal row as shown.

2. Sew the pieces together to make row 1. Repeat to make row 4.

3. Lay out 1 orange/brown 9-patch block, 1 pink/gray 9-patch block, 1 leaf/bird focal print setting triangle and (2) 1-1/2" x 9-1/2" cream solid sashing rectangle in a diagonal row as shown.

4. Sew the pieces together to make row 2. Repeat to make row 3.

5. Lay out rows 1-4 and 3 sashing rows as shown.

6. Sew the rows together. At this point, portions of the blocks and sashing will be " sticking out" .

7. Trim the runner center leaving a 1/4" seam allowance around all edges. The runner should measure approximately 14-3/4" x 43" from raw edge to raw edge.

Attaching the Borders

Inner border 1

Sew the 1-1/4" x 14-3/4" cream solid strips to opposite short sides of the runner center. Sew the 1-1/4" x 44-1/2" cream solid strips to the remaining sides of the runner center.

Inner border 2

Sew the 1" x 16-1/4" pink geometric print strips to opposite short sides of the runner center. Sew the 1" x 45-1/2" pink geometric print strips to the remaining sides of the runner center.

Outer border

Sew the 3" x 17-1/4" dark gray leaf print strips to opposite short sides of the runner center. Sew the 3" x 50-1/2" dark gray leaf print strips to the remaining sides of the runner center.

Finishing the Quilt

1. Lay the backing fabric, wrong side up on a flat surface. The backing fabric should be taut. Layer batting and runner top, right side up, on top of backing to form a quilt sandwich. Baste the quilt sandwich.

2. Quilt as desired.

3. Sew the (4) 2-1/4" -wide binding strips together along the short ends to make one continuous binding strip. Fold the piece in half lengthwise, wrong sides together, and press.

4. Square up the runner and attach binding and label to finish.

Credits:

1. Fabrics: RJR Fabrics - Flutter by Alex Anderson
2. Batting: Tuscany Silk Batt by Hobbs
3. Quilting Thread: Aurifil Mako 50 Cotton
4. Museum Collection: Illinois State Museum

Floral Fancy Wallhanging

Designed, pieced, appliquéd, quilted by Wendy Sheppard

Specification: intermediate

Finished size approximately: 34" square

I gave a Baltimore quilt block a contemporary look by using different shades of bright green (including lime) and red as the center of a table topper. Pieced patches in green frame the center block instead of the expected appliqué. An assortment of green fabrics was used for the leaves. The leaves are not arranged in a mirror-image manner, which gives a more informal touch. I also added scallops to the "bunting" appliqué, and combined two buntings for each corner of the quilt center.

The Daughters of the American Revolution Museum, Washington, DC

Gift of Jane Disharoon Bunting, Ann Disharoon Baker, and W. Robert Disharoon

Photo by Mark Gulezian/Quicksilver Photographers

Materials

1-1/8 yards solid white fabric

1-1/4 yards assorted green fabrics

5/8 yard assorted red fabrics

1/2 yard cream floral print fabric

3/8 yard red fabric

38" x 38" backing fabric

38" x 38" batting

Basic sewing supplies

Supplies for appliqué method of choice

Cutting Instructions

From solid white fabric, cut:

(1)   16-1/2" x 42" strip. From the strip, cut:
   (1) 16-1/2" square.
   From the remainder of the strip, cut:
   (4) 4-1/2" squares and
   (4) 4-1/2" x 8-1/2" rectangles.

(1)   4-1/2" x 42" strip. From the strip, cut:
   (8) 4-1/2" squares.

(2)   2-1/2" x 24-1/2" strips and
(2)   2-1/2" x 28-1/2" strips for inner border 1.

From assorted green fabrics, cut:

(4)   4-1/2" squares.

(4)   4-1/2" x 8-1/2" rectangles.

(2)   1" x 28-1/2" strips and
(2)   1" x 29-1/2" strips for inner border 2.

Urn, stem and leaf appliqué shapes using the templates on pages 84-85.

From assorted red fabrics, cut:

Flower, flower bud and bunting appliqué shapes using the templates on pages 84 and 86.

4 circles using the template on page 84.

From cream floral print fabric, cut:

(2)   3" x 29-1/2" strips and
(2)   3" x 34-1/2" strips for outer border.

From red fabric, cut:

(4)   2-1/4" -wide binding strips.

Assembling the Quilt Center

1. Draw a diagonal line on the wrong side of the 4-1/2" assorted green squares. Lay one of the marked squares on one corner of the 16-1/2" solid white square, right sides together. Sew on the drawn line. Trim 1/4" from the sewn line. Open and press to reveal green corner triangle.

2. In the same manner, sew the remaining 4-1/2" marked green squares to the remaining corners of the 16-1/2" solid white square. Press to complete a snowball block.

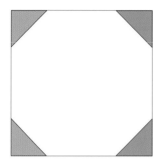

3. Draw a diagonal line on the wrong side of (8) 4-1/2" solid white squares. Lay one of the marked squares on one corner of a 4-1/2" x 8-1/2" assorted green rectangle, right sides together. Sew on the drawn line. Trim 1/4" from the sewn line. Open and press to reveal white corner triangle. Repeat with another 4-1/2" marked solid white square on the opposite corner of the 4-1/2" x 8-1/2" assorted green rectangle to complete 1 flying geese unit. Make a total of 4 flying geese units.

Make 4

4. Sew 4-1/2" solid white squares to opposite short sides of a flying geese unit. Make a total of 2 units.

Make 2

5. Sew the units made in step 4 to opposite sides of the snowball block.

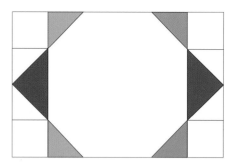

6. Sew 4-1/2" x 8-1/2" solid white rectangles to the opposite short sides of the 2 remaining flying geese units. Sew the units to the remaining sides of the snowball block to complete the quilt center.

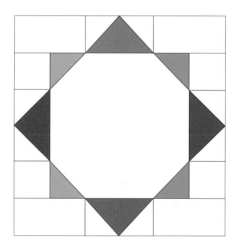

Note: If I am working with a smaller finished quilt like Floral Fancy, I prefer to have my quilt top completely pieced before adding appliqué. This way the appliqué block is set and I don't have to square it up after the appliqué pieces are added and finished on the block.

If you prefer, you can stitch the appliqué pieces on the quilt center before attaching the borders.

Attaching the Borders

Inner border 1

Sew the 2-1/2" x 24-1/2" solid white strips to the opposite sides of the quilt center. Sew the 2-1/2" x 28-1/2" solid white strips to the remaining sides of the quilt center.

Inner border 2

Sew the 1" x 28-1/2" assorted green strips to opposite sides of the quilt center. Sew the 1" x 29-1/2" assorted green strips to the remaining sides of the quilt center.

Outer border

Sew the 3" x 29-1/2" cream floral print strips to opposite sides of the quilt center. Sew the 3" x 34-1/2" cream floral print strips to the remaining sides of the quilt center to complete the quilt top.

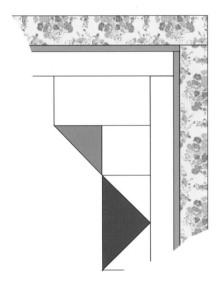

Adding the Appliqué

1. Prepare the appliqué pieces using your favorite method. Macine fusible appliqué was used on the Floral Fancy quilt. Referring to the photograph on page 78 and the placement diagram on page 87, arrange the prepared appliqué pieces on the quilt top.

2. Sew pieces in place using your favorite appliqué stitch. Floral Fancy was stitched with small blanket stitches. Refer to Appliqué Stitching Tips on page 83 for helpful hints on stitching the appliqué shapes.

Making the Yo-Yo Flowers

1. Finger-press the edges of the assorted red fabric circles a scant 1/8" to the wrong side of the fabric. Make running stitches close to the fold using one strand of thread.

2. Pull the strand of thread tight to create a gathered circle on the right side of the fabric. The back of the yo-yo should be flat. Knot the thread and bury it in the fold of the yo-yo. The finished yo-yos should measure 2" in diameter. Set the yo-yos aside.

Finishing the Quilt

1. Lay the backing fabric, wrong side up on a flat surface. The backing fabric should be taut. Layer batting and quilt top, right side up, on top of backing to form a quilt sandwich. Baste the quilt sandwich.

2. Quilt as desired.

3. Sew the (4) 2-1/4" -wide binding strips together along the short ends to make one continuous binding strip. Fold the piece in half lengthwise, wrong sides together, and press.

4. Square up quilt before attaching binding, yo-yo flowers, hanging sleeve and label.

Credits:

1. Fabrics: An assortment of Benartex and Art Gallery fabrics

2. Batting: Tuscany Silk Batt by Hobbs

3. Quilting Thread: Aurifil Mako 50 Cotton

4. Museum Collection: The Daughters of the American Revolution, Washington, DC

Appliqué Stitching Tips

Everyone has a favorite method when it comes to adding appliqué shapes to a project. My method of choice is blanket stitched, fusible machine appliqué.

I set my blanket stitch width and length between 1.4-1.6 on my machine. This creates teeny tiny stitches that are neat and tidy. For fabrics that tend to fray easily, I use 1.6. Otherwise, I try to set my stitches as small as possible. Tiny stitches do take more time to cover the territory, but it's worth the extra effort and time. You will need to play and experiment to find the stitch width and length that achieves the look you want.

Stitching with fine threads also makes my stitches look neater. I have used YLI Silk 100 and Aurifil Mako 50 Cotton with great results. I also like the fact that stitches created with the finer weight thread do not overpower the finished appliqué design. Once again, do not be afraid to experiment with a variety of threads to determine which works best for you.

My stitches penetrate about three threads into the fabric weave. I generally do not go more than three or four threads with the width penetration. With the shorter stitch length I am able to nicely follow the outline of the appliqué shapes using my open-toe foot.

Floral Fancy Wallhanging
Templates

*These templates have been reversed
for use with fusible appliqué*

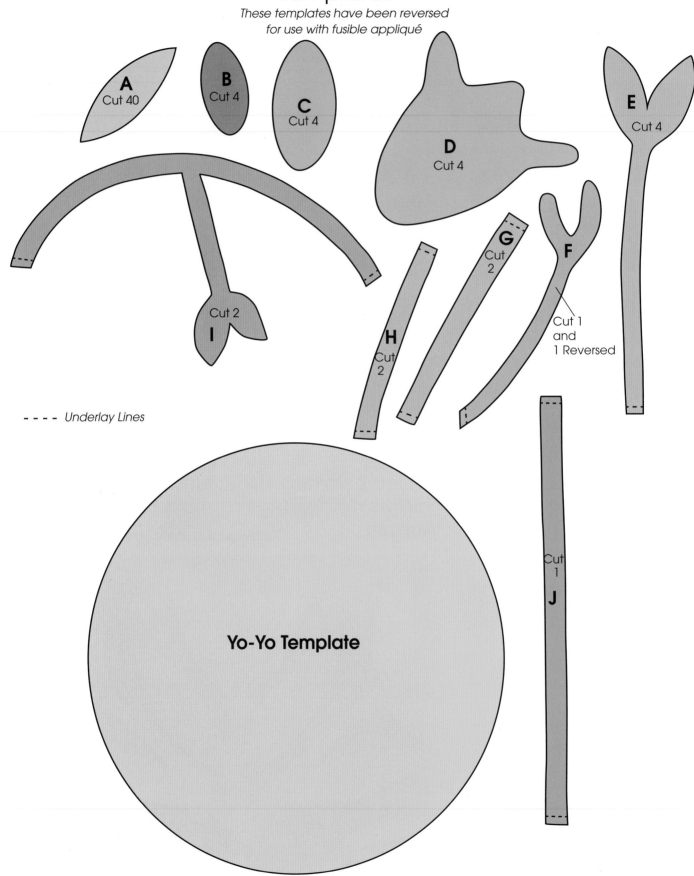

A
Cut 40

B
Cut 4

C
Cut 4

D
Cut 4

E
Cut 4

G
Cut 2

F
Cut 1
and
1 Reversed

I
Cut 2

H
Cut 2

- - - - *Underlay Lines*

J
Cut 1

Yo-Yo Template

Floral Fancy Wallhanging
Templates

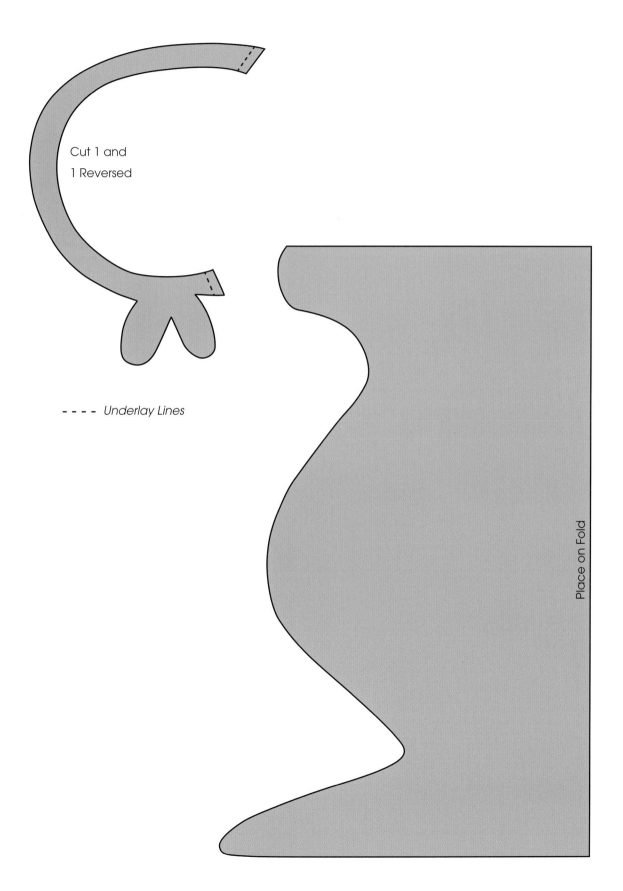

Cut 1 and
1 Reversed

- - - - *Underlay Lines*

Place on Fold

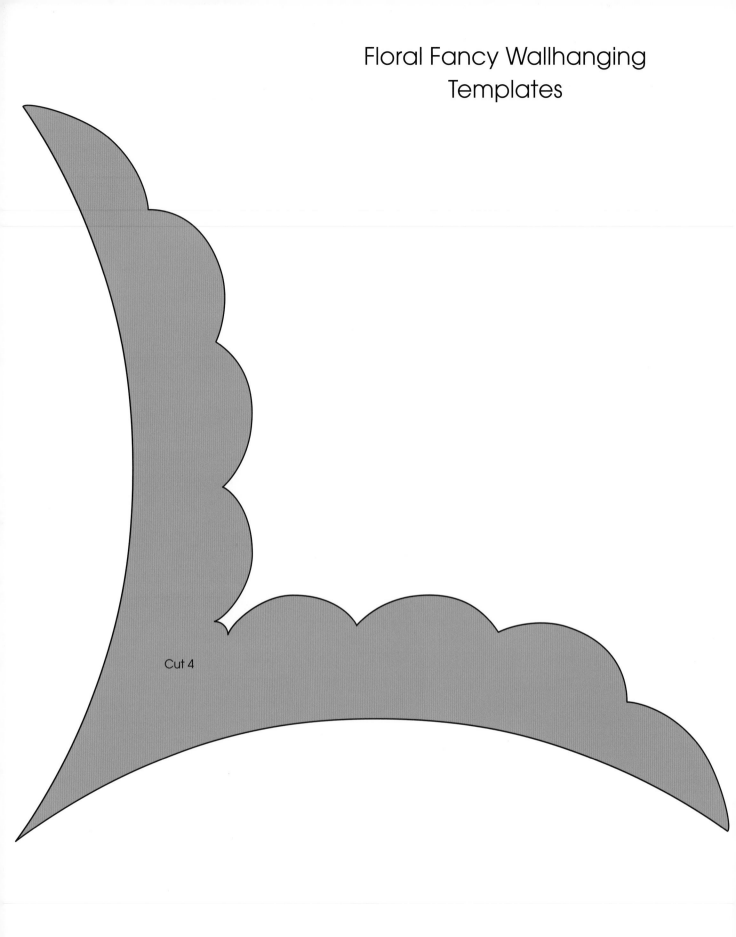

Cut 4

Floral Fancy Wallhanging
Placement Diagram

Ivory Baltimore Wallhanging

Designed, pieced, appliquéd, quilted by Wendy Sheppard

Specification: intermediate

Finished size approximately: 17" x 21"

The monochromatic color scheme of the Ivory Baltimore wallhanging was inspired by traditional French red/cream needlework samplers I admire. Instead of the usual red on cream, I decided to reverse the colors and did cream appliqué on a red background. Drawing on antique Quaker medallion samplers, where oftentimes the motifs were only stitched in half, I took one of the blocks from the DAR quilt and only appliquéd half of the block on the wallhanging.

The Daughters of the American Revolution Museum, Washington, DC

Gift of Jane Disharoon Bunting, Ann Disharoon Baker, and W. Robert Disharoon

Photo by Mark Gulezian/Quicksilver Photographers

Materials

3/8 yard scarlet tonal print fabric

1/2 yard cream mottled print fabric

5/8 yard coral solid fabric

21" x 25" backing fabric

21" x 25" batting

Basic sewing supplies

Supplies for appliqué method of choice

Cutting Instructions

From scarlet tonal fabric, cut:

(1)   7-1/2" x 21-1/2" strip.

From cream mottled fabric, cut:

(1)   1-1/2" x 21-1/2" strip.

Appliqué shapes using the templates on pages 92 and 94.

4 circles using the template on page 91.

From coral solid fabric, cut:

(1)   9-1/2" x 21-1/2" strip.

(3)   2-1/4" -wide binding strips.

Assembling the Quilt Top

1. Lay out the scarlet tonal, cream mottled and coral solid strips as shown.

2. Sew the strips together to complete the quilt top.

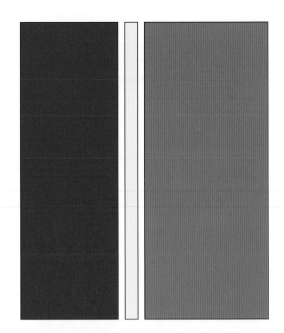

Adding the Appliqué

1. Mark a 1/4" seam allowance around the raw edge of the coral strip. Staying within the 1/4" marking, divide the strip into (3) 9" x 7" rectangular sections. Mark the sections using an erasable or washable marking tool.

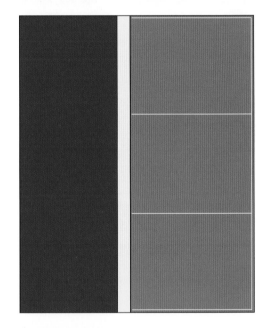

2. Prepare the appliqué pieces using your favorite method. Fusible machine appliqué was used on the Ivory Baltimore wallhanging. Referring to the photograph on page 88 and the placement diagrams on pages 93 and 94, arrange the prepared appliqué pieces on the wallhanging top. The appliqué in the coral section should be centered on the 9" x 7" rectangles.

3. Sew the pieces in place using your favorite appliqué stitch. Ivory Baltimore was stitched with small blanket stitches. Refer to Appliqué Stitching Tips on pages 83 for helpful hints on stitching the appliqué shapes.

Making the Yo-Yo Flowers

1. Finger-press the edges of the cream mottled fabric circles a scant 1/8" to the wrong side of the fabric. Make running stitches close to the fold using one strand of thread.

2. Pull the strand of thread tight to create a gathered circle on the right side of the fabric. The back of the yo-yo should be flat. Knot the thread and bury it in the fold of the yo-yo. The finished yo-yos should measure 2" in diameter. Set the yo-yos aside.

Finishing the Wallhanging

1. Lay the backing fabric, wrong side up on a flat surface. The backing fabric should be taut. Layer batting and wallhanging top, right side up, on top of backing to form a quilt sandwich. Baste the quilt sandwich.

2. Quilt as desired.

Quilting Notes: Tone-on-tone feather quilting gives the wallhanging a nice texture to highlight the cream on red appliqué.

3. Sew the (3) 2-1/4" -wide binding strips together along the short ends to make one continuous binding strip. Fold the piece in half lengthwise, wrong sides together, and press.

4. Square up the wallhanging before attaching binding, yo-yo flowers, hanging sleeve and label.

Credits:

1. Fabrics: Benartex - Electric Feathers
2. Batting: Tuscany Silk Batt by Hobbs
3. Quilting Thread: Aurifil Mako 50 Cotton
4. Museum Collection: The Daughters of the American Revolution, Washington, DC

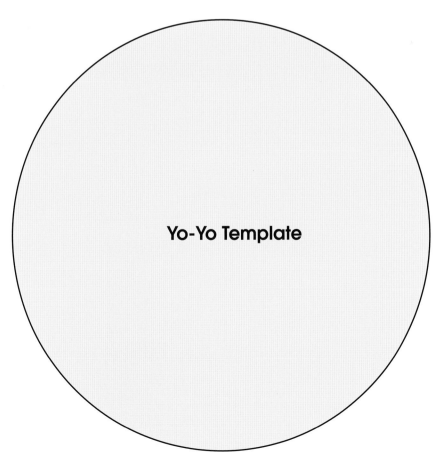

Yo-Yo Template

Ivory Baltimore Wallhanging
Templates

*These templates have been reversed
for use with fusible appliqué*

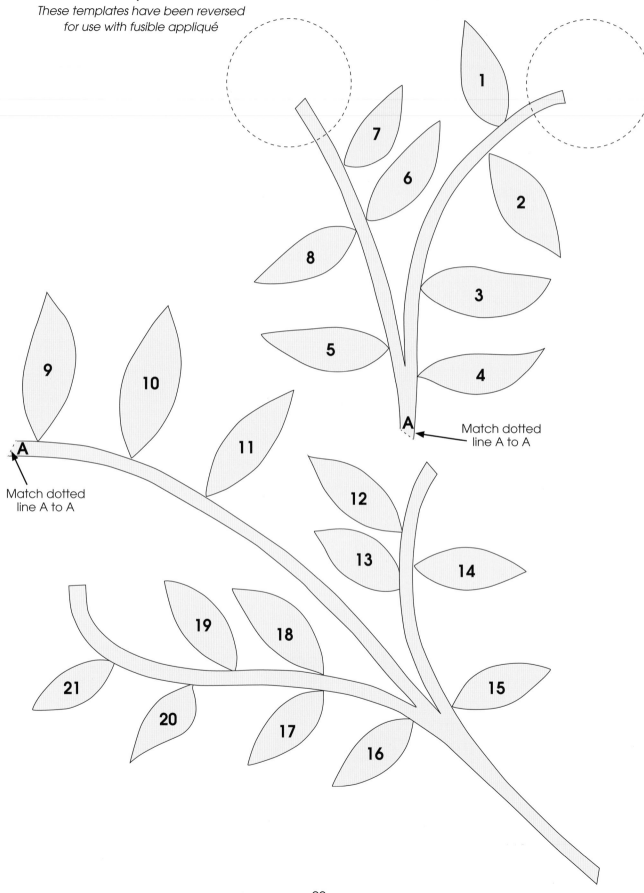

Match dotted
line A to A

Match dotted
line A to A

To Barbara Herring —my quilting teacher, mentor and friend. If she had insisted I make a four-patch beginner quilt for my first project, it's unlikely I would have progressed any further. Instead she patiently and graciously helped me through the intermediate pieced and appliquéd design I had chosen. Over the course of my quilting journey, Barbara remains a constant friend and mentor.

To Rogers Sewing Center - As a new quilter with no prior sewing experience, the wonderful people at Rogers Sewing Center, especially Dan Adams and Rhonda Guinn, have continually been a great source of encouragement and support.

To my blog friends - Quilters are some of the sweetest people on earth, including the many I have met online through my blog, ivoryspring. wordpress.com. Your friendships are priceless.

To the wonderful group at Landauer Publishing - This book would not have happened without the very capable editorial team at Landauer. I have thoroughly enjoyed working with all of you.

To Lisa—my sister who has never met a quilt project of mine she does not like. From the other end of the globe she is always available to chat and keep me awake when I work late into the night meeting deadlines.

To my little family - I am so appreciative of my husband Jason, who is unconditionally supportive in all my quilting endeavors. We are fortunate to have a remarkable 5-year-old daughter who understands when both her parents have to work hard to meet work-related deadlines. Gwendolyn often imagines herself a quilter in her playacting and thinks that rushing to the post office to ship a quilt is perfectly normal.

To my Lord and Savior, apart from Whom I am nothing. Soli Deo Gloria!

Special Thanks to the following for their generosity:
Fabrics: Art Gallery, Benartex, Quilting Treasures, RJR
Threads: Aurifil
Batting: Hobbs
Museums: Rutgers University Special Collections—The Heritage Quilt Project of New Jersey, Michigan State University, Illinois State Museum and The Daughters of the American Revolution, Washington, DC